THE
GASLIGHTING
RECOVERY
WORKBOOK

THE
GASLIGHTING
RECOVERY
WORKBOOK

Healing from Emotional Abuse

AMY MARLOW-MaCOY, LPC

ROCKRIDGE
PRESS

For general information on our other products and services or to obtain technical support, please contact our Customer Care Department within the U.S. at (866) 744-2665, or outside the U.S. at (510) 253-0500.

Rockridge Press publishes its books in a variety of electronic and print formats. Some content that appears in print may not be available in electronic books, and vice versa.

Interior and Cover Designer: Lisa Schreiber
Photo Art Director/Art Manager: Samantha Ulban
Editor: Shannon Criss
Production Editor: Ashley Polikoff
Author Photo: © Sahar Coston-Hardy

ISBN: Print 978-1-64611-269-2 | eBook 978-1-64611-270-8

R0

This book is dedicated to my amazing, resilient, and courageous clients. You inspire me daily with your bravery and commitment to healing.

CONTENTS

INTRODUCTION

✳ ✳ ✳

I will never forget the day Patti* walked into my office for her first therapy session and said, "I think I need to cut my father out of my life. He has been emotionally abusive for as long as I can remember, and I don't know what to do. Can you help me?"

When Patti started therapy, she was near her breaking point. She suffered from anxiety, perfectionism, and a nagging feeling she'd never be good enough. She was intelligent, insightful, and successful in her profession, but she still felt like a fraud. She found trusting her instincts difficult, though they were nearly always correct. As we explored her anxiety and lack of self-confidence, one thing became clear: She had experienced a phenomenon known as ***gaslighting*** for much of her life.

My name is Amy Marlow-MaCoy, and I am a licensed professional counselor. I support clients in recognizing, healing from, and building resilience to the effects of emotionally abusive relationships. Many of my clients come from homes where one or both parents demonstrated traits of narcissistic personality disorder or borderline personality disorder. Many have been gaslit into thinking their perceptions are warped and blame themselves for the abusive treatment they have received. In therapy, we work together to find the truth behind the lie of gaslighting.

Gaslighting is an emotional abuse tactic that makes the receiver doubt his or her perception of reality. In Patti's case, her father broke down her confidence by constantly questioning her judgment, downplaying or dismissing her achievements, and criticizing her emotional responses. He did these things, he told her, to help her become a stronger person. As a result, she eventually stopped relying on her own instincts and came to trust her father's perception more than her own. She came to me because as much as she wanted to be free of her father's abuse, she could not make that decision for herself.

A powerful tool for controlling others, gaslighting can be used to suppress or inflame whole communities within a larger society. Many leaders and politicians rely heavily on gaslighting to scapegoat certain groups or incite their own followers with skewed rhetoric. Because these personalities can be charming and charismatic, they can wield significant influence. With a strong enough following,

---

* All names have been changed to protect the identities of individuals.

a mob-like mentality can develop—one that can effectively silence anyone who steps outside the invisible lines.

While individuals with certain personality disorders, such as narcissistic personality disorder, borderline personality disorder, and antisocial personality disorder (also known as sociopathy), are more likely to engage in gaslighting to manipulate others, this tactic is not solely in the domain of narcissists and sociopaths. Individuals without personality disorders may also engage in gaslighting, although not always for the same reasons. Recognizing this as abuse can be hard initially, and calling out difficult behaviors you see in a close relationship even harder. We expect those closest to us to care for our well-being, and an expert gaslighter can make you believe he or she is hurting you for your own good.

As you become more aware of gaslighting across multiple settings and relationships, you may feel overwhelmed—maybe even hopeless. Survivors of emotional abuse often struggle with feelings of self-doubt, loss of confidence, anxiety, and depression, just to name a few. Fortunately, there is hope. You can learn to recognize the signs of gaslighting, and you can recover from the damage.

If you recognize yourself in the following pages, please know that recovery is possible for you, too. In reading, you will deepen your understanding of this sneaky form of emotional abuse, learn concrete skills to protect yourself from falling victim again, and begin to heal the wounds of the past. The courage and tenacity of my clients have inspired me to focus on supporting survivors of gaslighting, narcissistic abuse, and emotional manipulation. I am forever grateful to them for helping me discover my passion for this work. Now it's your turn to continue the legacy of healing.

HOW TO USE THIS BOOK

This workbook, divided into three parts, was created to bring the emotional abuse tactic known as gaslighting out into the open. Part I explores how to recognize signs of gaslighting, understand the goals of those who employ this tactic in relationships, and identify ways gaslighting may show up in different relationships and environments. Several exercises are geared toward helping you acknowledge your own experiences with gaslighting and develop self-compassion to begin your healing journey.

Parts II and III will walk you through exercises and prompts designed to build self-esteem, increase assertiveness, establish boundaries, and build healthier relationships. From start to finish, this workbook will help you establish a solid understanding of how gaslighting works, how to spot it, and how to recover.

While skipping straight to the exercises may be tempting, I strongly encourage you to start at the beginning and work your way through each section in order, as each chapter builds on the previous. You may find some exercises upsetting, while others you may want to revisit several times. **Please don't give up**. Sometimes the only way out is *through*, and healing is a work-through-it kind of endeavor. Be patient and kind to yourself.

If you find yourself feeling totally overwhelmed, traumatized, or hopelessly stuck in your healing process, consider seeking additional help. Healing from emotional abuse is hard work. A skilled and compassionate therapist can offer wonderful support.

Choosing the Right Therapist

So, you've decided to seek a therapist to help you heal? Congratulations! But where do you start?

When searching for the right therapist, consider such variables as license, education, therapeutic modalities, specialties, and cost. I recommend searching for a licensed psychotherapist, professional counselor, psychologist, or clinical social worker who specializes in recovery from emotional abuse and/or toxic relationships.

The Internet can be a useful tool to find the right person to help. A number of online registries list clinicians by location and areas of specialty. The Resources section at the end of this book (see page 169) also has a list of national registries. If you'd prefer to have a personal recommendation, ask friends or family members or your primary care doctor.

Finding a therapist who feels like a good fit for you personally is key. Many clinicians offer a brief, free telephone consultation before scheduling an initial session. Don't be afraid to ask prospective therapists about their experience helping clients recover from gaslighting and toxic relationships. And remember: It's okay to be picky. You deserve to find the right person to support you in your journey.

PART I

THE GASLIGHTING INFLUENCE

Gaslighting in a relationship can have a ripple effect across your life. The confusion, second-guessing, and disorientation caused by gaslighting impacts your engagement not only in the abusive relationship but with friends, family, loved ones, coworkers, and most importantly, yourself.

Gaslighting separates you from your anchors in life: your sense of self and your ability to trust yourself. Losing the connection to your own sense of reality makes you vulnerable to further abuse and increases your dependence on the gaslighter and the distorted reality they put forth. We begin the journey to recovery by helping you identify and understand the effects of gaslighting in your life.

CHAPTER 1

What Is Gaslighting?

Gaslighting is a form of psychological and emotional abuse that causes victims to question their reality, judgment, self-perception, and, in extreme circumstances, their sanity. Gaslighters distort truth to manipulate, confuse, and control their victims.

The term originates from Patrick Hamilton's 1938 play *Gas Light*, which was adapted into films in 1940 and 1944. The story features a man who manipulates and deceives his wife into believing she is going insane. One of the tactics he uses is to dim the gas lights in the home, making them flicker. When his wife asks about the lights, he convinces her that she has imagined the dimming. The 2001 movie *Amélie* also features a main character who gaslights someone—in this case, a shopkeeper. Amélie sneaks into his home and moves numerous objects around and programs his phone to dial a psychiatric institution when he thinks he's calling his mother. The shopkeeper is frightened and confused, and believes he has gone mad.

Gaslighting has taken on a broader definition in modern parlance. We now use the term to describe the tactic of manipulating victims into doubting their reality, memory, or perception. Changing the physical environment is not required; victims can be gaslit by questioning, mocking, or denying their reported experience until they lose confidence in their own senses.

A GASLIT SOCIETY

We live in an era of constant and nearly instantaneous fact-checking—as well as frequent claims of "fake news." While some stories are, indeed, fabricated, reality is not. When leaders and public figures make claims of falsehood against easily verifiable facts, they are engaging in gaslighting on a large scale. Even when presented with photographic, audio, or video evidence, a gaslighter will often claim that their words were taken out of context, misunderstood, or deliberately misconstrued. This practice is dangerous on many levels. Society-wide gaslighting can change the rules about what's right and wrong—what's moral and immoral. Gaslighting by powerful figures can effectively neutralize challengers by undermining their credibility, intellect, agency, and rationality.

Leaders may also gaslight their own followers, urging a kind of *groupthink* that discourages individuality and personal responsibility. This behavior is often done in the name of unity, patriotism, and loyalty to the leader. History is full of horrifying examples of the ways groupthink can push entire nations to hate, bigotry, and mass murder.

Gaslighting is not a new term, but has gained new life in the last several years. As a society, we are becoming increasingly aware of gaslighting in personal, professional, and political arenas. Those who have experienced gaslighting in one venue may be especially attuned to the signs of this pernicious form of emotional abuse in another. The good news is that the more we recognize the signs and symptoms of gaslighting, the more we can limit its potential for harm.

The Social Media and Advertising Effect

Social media venues offer the potential for gaslighting in ways previous generations never had to face. Now ubiquitous virtual communities and online networks have exploded in popularity in recent decades, beginning with the advent of AOL instant messaging, chat rooms, personal websites like MySpace and LiveJournal, and, of course, Facebook. Their reach is nothing short of staggering. Whereas twenty years ago, social media influencer was not an occupation, today a person can build an empire based on "likes."

Advertising can be a more covert form of gaslighting, particularly when its aim is to convince users to correct flaws they hadn't known they had. Presenting an image online that may not be congruent with reality is relatively easy. It can be as simple as altering an image with Photoshop. And there will always be those who deny editing their photos, despite clear and obvious evidence to the contrary. In the case of social media and advertising, then, trusting your own eyes can be deceptive. But sometimes when you look closely, you can see the distortion created by removing relevant facts and details. Discernment is crucial.

SIGNS OF GASLIGHTING

Gaslighting can occur in many different settings and types of relationships. While the themes of manipulation and control remain consistent, specific signs and symptoms may differ depending on the type of relationship. Throughout this book, we explore the ways gaslighting can show up in three different kinds of relationships: professional, romantic, and friends/family.

PROFESSIONAL

Gaslighting can occur between employees and managers or clients and employees, as well as among colleagues. Although more commonly seen from managers downward toward employees, gaslighting can occur in any professional relationship. Here are five common signs of gaslighting you may experience in the workplace:

You Become the Subject of Baseless Gossip

A gaslighting manager or coworker may attempt to tarnish your reputation through gossip, perhaps to more easily pin mistakes on you. The rumors and lies may have nothing to do with your work performance, and have no validity, but they will be presented as evidence of your unreliability and untrustworthiness. Gossip is difficult to fight since you'll rarely observe such hearsay directly.

You Are Persistently Discredited

The ultimate goal of a gaslighter is to rob you of credibility in your own mind as well as in the minds of others. Gaslighters may discredit you by arguing with, or undermining, your instructions. They may question your judgment or countermand your instructions to employees. And they don't even need to speak to devalue you in the office. An eye roll and a long-suffering stare can be as effective in implying your incompetence as any verbal comment.

You Are Expected to Read the Gaslighter's Mind

Gaslighting in the workplace can also occur when you are expected to somehow know what someone *really* wants, rather than what they *said* they wanted. Say you submit a project as requested, and your client complains you didn't add the details they wanted (but they didn't communicate these details to you). The client is gaslighting you for not reading their mind, which allows them to portray you to others as lazy, stupid, or uninspired.

You Are Treated Hypocritically

Hypocrisy may be one of the most infuriating faces of gaslighting in the workplace. The gaslighter may set a rule or hold you to a strict expectation they themselves do not uphold. Perhaps you are not allowed to show emotion during meetings, but your colleague flies into a rage when questioned. If you reacted similarly, you'd be written up or fired, but your colleague is excused as being "passionate."

You Are Often the Scapegoat

When workplace conflict arises, gaslighting can be used to scapegoat an employee, manager, or client as the sole source of the problem. A superior may report an employee as being insubordinate, while not acknowledging their own role in undermining, or lying about, the employee. A worker may also gaslight their superiors or colleagues by claiming to be punished unfairly without owning up to repeated lateness, unexcused absences, or failures to complete work projects.

Writing Exercise

Have you experienced signs of gaslighting in the workplace? Which signs have you seen, and how did they affect you at work?

_____

_____

_____

_____

_____

_____

_____

_____

_____

_____

ROMANTIC PARTNERS

You are most likely familiar with the term *toxic relationship*. One key factor in determining whether a relationship is healthy or toxic is the presence or absence of emotional abuse and manipulation. Gaslighting is common in toxic romantic relationships as an effective way for abusers to control their partners.

Let's look at some common signs of gaslighting in romantic relationships:

You Are Blatantly Lied to

Telling outright lies and simply denying a partner's experience is one form of gaslighting. This can include denying a behavior, despite clear evidence, or distorting the truth to make the victim look bad to outsiders. A gaslighter may also lie by creating a sad story to garner sympathy and divert a partner's anger, distress, or suspicions.

Your Partner Is Unfaithful

Gaslighting can show up as infidelity. In this case, a gaslighter may double down, laying responsibility for their behavior on you. Furthermore, a cheating partner may try to portray you as being irrationally jealous for showing anger or being hurt by their infidelity. To justify their choice to be unfaithful, a gaslighting partner will make you feel like no matter how much you give in a relationship, it's not enough.

You Are Pressured into Isolation

Isolation is a powerful and dangerous tool in the arsenal of an emotional abuser. A gaslighter may claim they are the only one who loves you enough to look past your flaws. They may criticize your friends and family, saying they "just don't like" the gaslighter, and exaggerate or simply make up supporting evidence for their assertions. Isolating you makes control of you easier, preventing the opportunity for you to gain needed perspective.

You Are Bullied or Intimidated

When all else fails, a gaslighter may resort to openly bullying to maintain power. They may make veiled or open threats against you, your pets, or your children. They may threaten to lie to your boss or get you arrested on frivolous or false charges unless you do what they want. Bullying can also take place online, through harassing emails and phone calls, or by stalking.

You Are Accused of Malicious Intent

Another way of keeping victims off-balance in a romantic relationship is to ascribe malicious intent to innocent and innocuous events. You may think you're both harmlessly teasing each other until your gaslighter suddenly turns on you, accusing you of cruelty or mean-spirited jabs. They may claim you deliberately provoked them or accuse you of using your own fear or surprised reaction to manipulate them.

Writing Exercise

Have you experienced gaslighting in a romantic relationship? What signs have you noticed, and how have they affected your relationship?

_____

_____

_____

_____

_____

_____

_____

_____

_____

Friends and family can be the bedrock of our lives, or the jackhammer that cracks the ground on which we stand. We all have certain expectations of how close personal relationships should work. Loyalty to loved ones is both ingrained as instinct and held as an important social value. We expect those closest to us to care about our well-being and treat us with love and respect. Gaslighters may use these expectations against you. They may pressure you to put loyalty to the relationship above your own judgment, perception, and needs. Or they may imply you were foolish to expect love and respect from those closest to you.

Let's look at some common signs of gaslighting in relationships with friends and family:

You Are Made to Feel Guilty

Guilt trips are a surefire way for friends and family to pressure you into falling in line with expectations. Friends and family may gaslight you by making you feel as if you've done something wrong though you haven't. If you feel guilty, you are more likely to bow to the wishes of the abuser to appease them, or to make up for your supposed wrongdoing.

You Are Treated as Though You Are Overreacting

Confronting a gaslighter about a problematic behavior can trigger defensiveness. They will often avoid taking responsibility for their behavior by justifying and defending what they've done. The implication is that you are overreacting, or even attacking them. Treating confrontation as an attack allows them to rationalize their response as standing up for themselves.

You Are Made to Feel Your (Reasonable) Request Is Onerous and Unfair

Treating a reasonable request as something onerous and unfair implies you are being demanding and unappreciative. In these instances, the gaslighter is playing the martyr to suppress your attempts to advocate for your own needs. By letting you know just how much your request will require of them, a gaslighter wants you to feel ashamed for asking.

You Are Blamed and Shamed

Blaming and shaming places all responsibility for one person's behavior on another's actions. This situation is particularly common in cases of domestic violence, where the aggressor will often blame the victim for provoking them into violence. The gaslighter absolves themselves of any responsibility for their behavior and persuades the victim that they, the victim, deserved to be abused.

You Suffer Retaliation

Gaslighting can be employed as retaliation for normal behavior that reflects independence and autonomy. Take, for example, a young adult who decides to celebrate a birthday out with friends rather than with family. Gaslighting parents might respond to such a developmentally appropriate desire by going "scorched earth," rejecting them from *all* family functions. Being shut out of family events and dynamics can be devastating, especially if your intention was not to end a relationship but simply to ask for a little breathing room.

Writing Exercise

Have you experienced gaslighting by a friend or family member? How has this experience affected your relationship and self-perception?

_____

_____

_____

_____

_____

_____

_____

_____

_____

_____

_____

_____

_____

_____

SIDE EFFECTS OF GASLIGHTING

Gaslighting can have lasting effects in many areas of a victim's life. Read each description below, and check each that applies to you.

☐ **Lack of Confidence/Self-Esteem**

Because gaslighting works by making victims question their own perceptions, thought processes, and conclusions, victims often develop low self-confidence. Victims are made to feel that they are wrong if they question or disagree with the gaslighter.

☐ **Unhappiness/Loss of Joy**

Being repeatedly corrected, invalidated, or dismissed can drain the joy from self-expression. When gaslighting is employed to control or manipulate another person, the victim may feel stifled and constrained. They may begin to conclude they can't get anything right and will never live up to someone else's expectations. This way of thinking can lead to feelings of sadness, as well as a loss of excitement about sharing their insights and experiences.

☐ **Unnecessarily Apologetic**

Victims of gaslighting share a tendency to apologize when they haven't actually done anything wrong. Some abusers will project responsibility for their own feelings or actions onto their victims; when they accept this blame, victims feel overly responsible for things outside their control. They may apologize unnecessarily for having an opinion, for minor mistakes, or for not being available for social plans or events.

☐ **Indecisive**

Victims of gaslighting often struggle to make decisions and may constantly second-guess their choices. "Are you sure that's what you want?" may sound like an innocuous question to many, but it can be paralyzing to a victim of gaslighting. Someone on the receiving end of gaslighting often has been shamed or ridiculed to the point they have a hard time accepting and owning their wishes. They may agonize over even simple decisions, fearful of upsetting someone with their choice.

☐ **Confused**

The power of gaslighting lies in causing victims to feel confused about what they believe and feel. Gaslighters create confusion by challenging a victim's character, knowledge, feelings, and/or sensory experiences and replacing them with their own. Sorting out one's own thoughts and feelings while being pressed to accept someone else's is disorienting. Gaslighters create and take advantage of this confusion to keep victims off-balance and unsure of themselves.

☐ **Full of Self-Doubt**

Repeated gaslighting causes victims to doubt their sensory input, feelings, and judgments. The result is often feeling ignorant, uninformed, and misguided, or perhaps even questioning their own intentions. Self-doubt discourages the victim from challenging the gaslighter, thereby keeping them under the abuser's control.

☐ **Anxious**

Victims of frequent gaslighting may experience constant, low-level anxiety with no clear cause and may need to repeatedly check their work or ask others to do so. Anxiety may persist even when gaslighting is not happening in the moment. Experiencing anticipatory anxiety, plagued by worry about future events and situations, is also common.

☐ **Denying Gaslighting Behavior in Another**

One reason gaslighting is so effective is that abusers convince their victims they are acting out of love or a sincere desire to help. This tactic creates a sense of gratitude and obligation in victims, who then feel they cannot ascribe negative intentions to the gaslighter. Victims of gaslighting may refuse to accept any evidence that the gaslighter is being abusive, believing the gaslighter's lie that they "just want to help."

☐ Depressed

Sometimes the aforementioned unhappiness and loss of joy goes deeper, especially when gaslighting is prolonged and personal. Victims may become depressed and hopeless, believing themselves to be fundamentally flawed. They may fall into despair, fearing they may never be good enough or ever "get it right." The victim may become depressed and conclude their situation is as good as it gets, and stop expecting things to improve.

☐ Extremely Stressed

In situations of severe emotional abuse, gaslighting may provoke extreme stress in victims. In the play and film versions of *Gas Light*, the wife becomes extremely distressed by her husband's insistence she is losing her sanity. The stress can be incapacitating, leaving victims vulnerable to further abuse and dependent upon their gaslighter to tell them what is real, drawing them further into the cycle of abuse.

Writing Exercise

Which effect resonates most with you? How does this side effect show up in your life?

_____

_____

_____

_____

_____

_____

_____

_____

_____

_____

_____

_____

_____

_____

_____

CHAPTER 2

The Gaslighter

I n this chapter, we profile individuals most known for gaslighting. This form of emotional abuse is commonly associated with mental illnesses such as narcissistic personality disorder, borderline personality disorder, and antisocial personality disorder. The Diagnostic and Statistical Manual of Mental Disorders, Fifth Edition (DSM-5, 2013) defines a personality disorder as "an enduring pattern of inner experience and behavior that deviates markedly from the expectations of the individual's culture." Problematic traits and behaviors are persistent and dysfunctional. As a result, these individuals both suffer and cause pain to others, disrupting their lives and relationships.

Some people may demonstrate traits that do not meet criteria for a mental health diagnosis. A useful term for not-quite-diagnosable individuals is *almost psychopaths*. Almost psychopaths can charm, manipulate, and bully with the best, but stop short of a true mental illness. Anyone can be abusive, but not everyone who abuses has a personality disorder.

PROFILE OF THE ABUSER

Gaslighting can be a symptom of several personality disorders. According to the National Institute of Mental Health, about 9% of adults meet criteria for a personality disorder diagnosis. Though gaslighting is not a clear indication of a personality disorder—and plenty of gaslighters do not have a mental health diagnosis—individuals with (diagnosed or not) personality disorders are very likely to practice gaslighting in many relationships. Here, we will focus on gaslighting as an extension of certain, more commonly diagnosed personality disorders.

NARCISSISTIC PERSONALITY DISORDER

A personality disorder is a collection of personality traits that persist across relationships and environments, causing pain and distress in those relationships. Individuals with narcissistic personality disorder often express traits like an attitude of grandiosity, excessive need for admiration, lack of empathy and insight, constant need for praise, a belief that they are special and deserving of special treatment, coercive and manipulative behaviors, and a tendency to bully others to get their own way.

Those with this personality disorder take advantage of others, manipulating and making use of the people around them for their own benefit. Narcissists may use gaslighting to maintain their own sense of superiority by keeping others in a disempowered position. Many political figures and CEOs are high in narcissistic traits. These authority figures may use gaslighting to either inflame their admirers or suppress their opposition, pursuing their personal agendas at the expense of the well-being of others.

BORDERLINE PERSONALITY DISORDER

Borderline personality disorder is characterized by heightened emotional reactivity, intense fear of rejection, instability in interpersonal relationships, and a sense of emptiness at their core. This disorder also includes a tendency to cycle between idealizing and devaluing loved ones, pulling them closer and pushing them away.

Individuals with borderline personality disorder will go to great lengths to avoid real or perceived abandonment, including threatening to harm themselves if their partner tries to leave. They may utilize gaslighting to make others feel responsible for the gaslighter's welfare. In this case, gaslighting is less about trying to intentionally control another person than about trying to meet the borderline person's own need to feel secure.

OTHER SOCIOPATHIC DISORDERS

Those with antisocial personality disorder and psychopathy are also likely culprits of gaslighting. Antisocial personality disorder, sometimes called sociopathy, is characterized by a disregard for, or violating, the rights of others. Sociopathic individuals do not conform to social norms. They are likely to gaslight by way of lying or deception, and they may direct harmful behavior toward strangers rather than loved ones.

Although the terms are sometimes used interchangeably, sociopathic and psychopathic traits differ in intensity and targeting. Sociopathic individuals are less likely to deliberately target those closest to them, while psychopathic individuals are equally likely to display harmful behavior to family, friends, or strangers. Psychopathic individuals are similarly unconcerned with the consequences of their actions but are incapable of empathy or remorse. They may actually enjoy hurting other people.

GOALS OF GASLIGHTING

Abusers use gaslighting to control their victims, across all settings and types of relationships. Five pathological goals of gaslighters are:

DISABLE DISCERNMENT IN THE VICTIM

Gaslighting creates doubt and confusion for the victim. Because the victim questions their own judgement and perceptions, they may find it difficult to differentiate right from wrong, healthy from unhealthy, their perspective from their abuser's perspective. Gaslighting makes victims feel like they can't trust themselves to discern the truth of a situation. They become more and more dependent on the gaslighter for a "reality check," which only serves to perpetuate their confusion.

SILENCE THE VICTIM

Abuse thrives in silence and secrecy. Gaslighting can be an effective tool to silence someone by making them doubt their own credibility. Abusers will diminish the influence and reach of their victim's voice through lying and discrediting. They may convince the victim that no one will believe them because they (the victim) are such an unreliable witness.

ESTABLISH A SENSE OF ENTITLEMENT OVER THE VICTIM

Abusers manipulate victims into abandoning their own reality, forcing them to accept the abuser's version. Gaslighters replace their victim's perceptions with their own by using "alternative facts." Gaslighters do not value their victim's point of view. Instead, they value feeling powerful, admired, and in control. Abusers steamroll their victims because they feel entitled to change someone else's reality rather than question their own.

DEGRADE AND CHASTISE THE VICTIM

Gaslighters may degrade and devalue victims by portraying the victim's emotional response to abuse as childish or immature. Chastising a victim for reacting to provocation implies that the fault lies with the victim, not the abuser. Abusers may also degrade their victims by downplaying the victim's successes or achievements. The gaslighter may chastise the victim for feeling pride, suggesting that if the victim worked hard enough, they would actually have something to show that's *really* worth that pride.

LEGITIMIZE THEIR TREATMENT OF THE VICTIM

Gaslighting can be used to convince the victim that the perpetrator's abusive behavior is warranted. As faith in their own faculties decreases, they become more reliant on and accepting of the gaslighter's reality. And when a victim believes they deserve the treatment they receive, they become less likely to resist or challenge problematic behaviors. Additionally, the gaslighter may convince themselves that they are behaving harshly for the victim's benefit and that this treatment is justified.

Writing Exercise

Emotional abuse in the form of gaslighting is effective because it systematically breaks down the victim's confidence, autonomy, and self-efficacy. The five goals identified in the previous section place the gaslighter in more control of their victim. How have the gaslighter(s) in your life pursued these goals in your relationship? Write about your experiences with each of their five goals.

_____

_____

_____

_____

_____

_____

_____

_____

Common Phrases Used by a Gaslighter

Below are several common gaslighting phrases. If any sound familiar, place a check in the adjacent box.

☐ "I wouldn't have said that if you hadn't provoked me." Here, the gaslighter deflects blame onto the victim. The goal is to make the victim believe they brought the abuse upon themselves.

☐ "You deliberately misinterpreted what I said." This phrase casts blame on the victim for not reading the gaslighter's mind and implies the victim distorted the gaslighter's "innocent" intent.

☐ "You know how I feel about that and you did it anyway, so the way I've reacted is your own fault." This phrase implies the victim antagonized the gaslighter, justifying their abusive behavior in response.

☐ "That never happened." Denying a victim's memories and experiences confuses and disorients them. Gaslighters also discredit victims to others by denying events or claiming to have no memory of them.

☐ "You sound crazy." Rejecting someone's feelings or beliefs as sounding crazy triggers self-doubt and anxiety in victims.

☐ "You're trying to confuse me." This accusation reverses the position of the abuser and victim, putting the true victim on the defensive.

☐ "I have no idea what you're talking about." Claiming not to understand a victim's concern suggests that their experience is so far out of the norm, it's unintelligible. The victim then questions whether they are imagining things or if their memory is skewed.

☐ "You're remembering it wrong." This phrase implies that the victim's memories and perceptions are unreliable, calling their judgment into question.

☐ "I am only hard on you because I love you." This phrase is used to engender gratitude and forgiveness in victims. Abusers claim to believe in "tough love," or "telling it like it is," regardless of the impact on the other person.

☐ "You are too sensitive. You need to grow a thicker skin." Perhaps one of the most insidious phrases in the gaslighting catalog, the thinking behind these words calls into question the victim's right to their own feelings. If the victim is "too sensitive," the onus is on the victim to learn to tolerate the abuse, rather than on the gaslighter to stop what they're doing.

UNDERSTANDING GASLIGHTING BEHAVIOR

Now that you're familiar with the signs and goals of gaslighting, you'll be better able to avoid falling prey to it in the future. Looking back at your past and seeing the manipulation in a relationship you once thought was love can be hard. You might wonder why you couldn't see through the manipulation at the time, and why you had to suffer so much pain before you realized what was really happening. You may feel damaged, broken, or stupid for having been victimized. Be kind to yourself. Being targeted by an abusive personality is not a character flaw.

Abusers target victims based on one of two things: vulnerability and desirability. Some gaslighters look for victims who are willing to overlook poor treatment and abusive behavior. They target people who want to be perceived as agreeable and easy to be with; these individuals are less likely to call the gaslighter out and are more easily manipulated. There is such a thing as being too nice, and gaslighters will take advantage of that to manipulate victims.

Abusers may also target individuals who appear confident, successful, wealthy, or attractive. They are drawn to strong, confident people. Manipulators draw people in through a process called "lovebombing"—showering potential victims with affection, praise, and psuedo-intimacy. Once victims are hooked, the gaslighting begins and abusers begin to break down the confidence that first drew them to their target.

Profile of a Gaslightee

Are some personality types more susceptible to being gaslit than others? While abusers target victims for different reasons, many victims do have some traits in common. Many gaslightees are people-pleasers, overly concerned with being polite, agreeable, or well-liked. They are conscientious, concerned with others' feelings, and may feel guilty saying "no." Finally, gaslightees are likely to excuse or overlook rude and hurtful behavior to an excessive degree.

Do you fit the gaslightee profile? Take the self-test below:

GASLIGHTEE SELF-TEST

Rate how true each statement is for you by circling "Often true," "Sometimes true," or "Rarely true."

1. Disagreeing with someone feels like I am "starting drama." I try to avoid these types of situations.

    Often true   Sometimes true   Rarely true

2. I worry that I will hurt someone's feelings if I say "no" to them.

    Often true   Sometimes true   Rarely true

3. I respect other people's opinions more than my own.

    Often true   Sometimes true   Rarely true

4. If I am doing well and my partner is not, I feel like my success is hurting them.

    Often true   Sometimes true   Rarely true

5. I feel like I should be more in control of my emotions.

    Often true   Sometimes true   Rarely true

If you answered "often true" to more than three questions, you may be at a higher risk of being gaslit. Remember, your voice and opinions matter, and it's okay to say "no." You have a right to be treated with respect.

PART II

STAGES OF RECOVERY

Recovery from emotional abuse is a process. Much like building a house starts with laying a solid foundation, recovery from gaslighting begins with coming to terms with the painful reality that you have experienced abuse in a relationship. In phase one of your recovery, acknowledgment and self-compassion, you identify, explore, and come to terms with the ways gaslighting has manifested itself in your life. The road to healing begins with acknowledging the existence of a wound, followed by developing a mind-set of kindness toward yourself.

CHAPTER 3

Phase One (Acknowledgment and Self-Compassion)

Now that we have laid the groundwork, you are ready to begin your journey to gaslighting recovery. We've talked about what gaslighting is, how this behavior may appear in various settings, and what makes gaslighting damaging in relationships. We have also covered the signs and side effects of gaslighting, as well as what prompts people to employ this abusive tactic. Now it's your turn. You will begin to explore and acknowledge the ways gaslighting has affected you personally.

This chapter contains a number of exercises and journal prompts to help you understand manipulation in unhealthy relationships. The first step in your recovery is recognizing, and allowing yourself to admit, you've been a victim of gaslighting. Acknowledging the truth by naming what's happened can help demystify a confusing experience. The first part of this chapter will focus on helping you through this process as you review past and current relationships.

Acknowledging you have experienced emotional abuse may bring up feelings of shame. Gaslighting damages your self-esteem and distorts your self-perception. For this reason, learning to practice self-compassion is critical to your recovery. Self-compassion is a mind-set. With self-compassion you offer yourself kindness, understanding, and recognition of the pain you have suffered, without criticism or self-blame. Beating yourself up for being manipulated will not help you heal the wounds of an abusive relationship. Bringing kindness and compassion to the parts of you that have been hurt will.

Let's begin!

RECOGNIZING MANIPULATION

Do you know gaslighting when you see it? In the following vignettes, you will have three opportunities to identify elements of gaslighting in real-life settings. Read each story carefully, and see if you can spot the signs and side effects of gaslighting in each scenario—review the "Signs of Gaslighting" and "Side Effects of Gaslighting" sections in chapter 1, if needed (see pages 5 through 11).

CRUSHED HOPES

Julia is excited to move into her first college dormitory and start a new, independent, adult life. She eagerly tells her mom about her plans to play an intramural sport. "I feel really ready to start something new!" she gushes. When her mother laughs aloud, Julia is crushed.

"Oh, honey," she says condescendingly, "you know you aren't athletic enough for sports." Julia feels her excitement and confidence drain away. She had thought intramurals would be a fun way to develop a new skill, but now she isn't sure. "Sorry, Mom. I guess you're right. I was probably being silly. Thanks for the reality check."

Identify the Signs and Side Effects

1. Identify two to three signs of gaslighting in this interaction.

_____

_____

_____

2. Identify two to three side effects of gaslighting Julia is experiencing.

_____

_____

_____

_____

3. Have you ever experienced a friend or family member gaslighting your interests, skills, or plans? Write about this experience here.

_____

_____

_____

_____

Andre has discovered a flirtatious and sexually explicit text between his partner, Ben, and another man. Andre and Ben have had this fight many times in the past. Andre is hurt and angry. He confronts Ben. He tells Ben that the relationship is over, and he is moving out.

"I can't believe you are being so dramatic over a couple of text messages," Ben complains, sounding disgusted. "I am not cheating on you. You're just seeing what you want to see. Why are you so suspicious? You love to be the victim, and I'm not going to put up with it. You don't get to control me." Ben turns away from Andre, the picture of wounded pride. Andre is devastated.

"Ben, I didn't mean to accuse you of cheating. I just got so upset when I saw the texts. I'm sorry I attacked you. I just want us to be honest with each other." Andre puts his arms around Ben and whispers a contrite, "I'm sorry. I love you." Ben turns to Andre and hugs him back. "I forgive you."

Identify the Signs and Side Effects

1. Identify two to three signs of gaslighting in this interaction.

_____

_____

_____

_____

2. Identify two to three side effects of gaslighting that Andre is experiencing.

_____

_____

_____

_____

3. Have you ever experienced gaslighting by a romantic partner? Write about this experience here.

_____

_____

_____

_____

_____

Gaslighting in a Vulnerable Population

Although anyone can be hurt by emotional abuse, some populations have a greater risk of serious harm. Individuals who identify as asexual, gender nonbinary, queer, or transgender have additional risk factors, as their emotional abuse can be compounded by existing societal beliefs and power structures. LGBTQ individuals may be gaslit by others questioning their "queerness," denying use of the correct pronoun, or convincing them they deserve abuse because of their sexuality and gender identity.

OFFICE GOSSIP

Sasha is looking forward to her upcoming performance evaluation. She has worked hard in her new position and has been very productive. She has a good rapport with her supervisor, Felicia, and left their pre-evaluation meeting with a positive impression. Felicia even hinted at the possibility of a performance-based raise.

When Felicia calls Sasha into her office to go over the evaluation, Sasha is shocked and dismayed to read Felicia's notes: "Sasha's overall performance is disappointing. She does not put in exceptional effort but feels entitled to a raise. Sasha needs to reset her expectations and improve her work ethic if she wants to progress in this company."

As she reads the comments, Sasha feels confused and humiliated. She wonders if she was reading into Felicia's earlier comments about a possible raise, and if she made herself look greedy by showing excitement at the prospect. Later, she overhears two managers from other departments discussing her. Felicia has told them that Sasha demanded a raise and complained about her colleagues. The gossip is spreading like wildfire, and Sasha finds herself increasingly shunned by coworkers.

Identify the Signs and Side Effects

1. Identify two to three signs of gaslighting in this interaction.

_____

_____

_____

_____

_____

_____

2. Identify two to three side effects of gaslighting Sasha is experiencing.

_____

_____

_____

_____

_____

_____

3. Have you ever experienced gaslighting in the workplace? Write about this experience here.

_____

_____

_____

_____

_____

_____

_____

Spotting the Signs in Real Life

Review the "Signs of Gaslighting" section in chapter 1 (see pages 5 through 8). Write an example of how each sign has shown up in your life. It's okay if your experiences don't exactly line up with the settings in the list (e.g., you may have been bullied by a friend or scapegoated by a sibling).

I have been the subject of baseless gossip.

_____

_____

_____

_____

_____

I have been persistently discredited.

_____

_____

_____

_____

I have been expected to read someone's mind.

_____

_____

_____

_____

_____

I have been treated hypocritically.

_____

_____

_____

_____

_____

I have been the scapegoat.

_____

_____

_____

_____

I have been blatantly lied to.

_____

_____

_____

_____

_____

_____

I have been cheated on.

_____

_____

_____

_____

_____

_____

I have been pressured to isolate myself from family and friends.

_____

_____

_____

_____

_____

_____

I have been bullied or intimidated.

_____

_____

_____

_____

I have been accused of malicious intent where there was none.

_____

_____

_____

_____

_____

I have been made to feel guilty.

_____

_____

_____

_____

_____

I have been treated as though I were overreacting.

_____

_____

_____

_____

_____

I have been made to feel like my reasonable request to another was onerous or unfair.

_____

_____

_____

_____

_____

I have been blamed and shamed.

_____

_____

_____

_____

_____

Someone has retaliated against me.

_____

_____

_____

_____

_____

Identifying Your Side Effects

Review the "Side Effects of Gaslighting" section found in chapter 1 (see pages 9 through 11). Write an example of how each of these side effects has shown up in your life.

I have lacked confidence or had low self-esteem.

_____

_____

_____

_____

_____

I have experienced unhappiness or a loss of joy.

_____

_____

_____

_____

_____

I have found myself apologizing for things outside my own control or for situations in which I had a right to say "no."

_____

_____

_____

_____

_____

I have felt indecisive.

_____

_____

_____

_____

_____

_____

I have felt confused.

_____

_____

_____

_____

_____

I have been full of self-doubt.

_____

_____

_____

_____

I have been persistently anxious.

_____

_____

_____

_____

_____

I have been in denial of another's gaslighting behavior.

_____

_____

_____

_____

_____

_____

I have felt depressed.

_____

_____

_____

_____

_____

_____

I have felt extremely stressed.

_____

_____

_____

_____

_____

Bonus

If any of these side effects *used* to be applicable but no longer are, what has changed? Write about how you made the change.

_____

_____

_____

_____

_____

_____

_____

_____

Hindsight is 20/20: Reviewing Past Incidents

Looking over past incidents of gaslighting can help you recognize them in the future. Write about a time you experienced gaslighting. Identify the thoughts and feelings you experienced at the time, as well as any lingering thoughts and feelings you presently have.

Choose an example of gaslighting in your life. Write about this experience in as much detail as you can.

How did you feel when the gaslighting situation happened?

_____

_____

_____

_____

_____

_____

_____

How do you feel about this incident now?

_____

_____

_____

_____

_____

What kinds of thoughts did you have at the time?

_____

_____

_____

_____

_____

_____

What kinds of thoughts do you have about this incident now?

_____

_____

_____

_____

_____

If you encountered this situation today, what would you want to do differently? Write how you would like to respond now that you know more about gaslighting.

_____

_____

_____

_____

Copy the preceding two pages and repeat this exercise as often as you'd like. And don't hesitate to revisit an event more than once. You may learn new things about the same or similar situations by repeating the exercise.

Where Have I Seen This Behavior Before?

Make a list of movies, television shows, plays, or books where you can identify gaslighting. Are there any you wouldn't have noticed before starting this book?

_____

_____

_____

_____

_____

_____

_____

_____

Your Body in Space

Take a moment to notice your body. How do you stand? Do you stand tall, or are your shoulders slumped? Do you make yourself as small as possible around other people, or are you comfortable taking up space?

Men, women, and gender nonbinary individuals alike have experienced gaslighting related to their physical bodies through social media, advertising, and perhaps other types of venues. Perhaps you were happy with your body until your social media feed suddenly filled with shapewear ads. Or you were content being slender until you got bombarded with commercials for protein powder and bodybuilding programs. Lack of pop culture and media representation (or misrepresentation) of persons with physical challenges, of color, or with a sexual identity that varies from the mainstream can send a message about forms of personal identity and self-expression that are socially acceptable, and those that are portrayed as deviant, non-normative, or caricatures.

Think about what you have been told about your body and physical presence in the world. Answer the questions below to explore ways you may have experienced gaslighting when it comes to your body.

When I think about my body and my appearance, I feel:

_____

_____

_____

_____

Where did I learn to think this way about my body?

_____

_____

_____

_____

Something I accept and love about my body (even if someone implies I should not) is:

_____

_____

_____

_____

_____

Did you know that traumatic experiences can affect our bodies, not just our minds? In his seminal work, *The Body Keeps the Score* (2014), Dr. Bessel Van der Kolk explores ways trauma can cause changes to brain functioning, elevate nervous system arousal, and cause long-term pain and chronic illness. Your body does not differentiate between trauma that comes from military combat or emotional abuse such as gaslighting. Trauma is trauma, and our bodies can tell the story of our emotional pain.

As we move through this chapter and begin to focus on self-compassion, don't forget about your body. Pay attention to physical sensations that may arise as you work through this book. Persistent headaches, nausea, fatigue, a racing heart, and clenched fists can all be indicators of trauma being expressed through your body. If you notice these symptoms during an exercise, try to pause and thank your body. Although uncomfortable, these physical sensations are giving you more information about how and where trauma is stored in your body.

EMBODIED FEELINGS MEDITATION

Find somewhere that feels quiet, peaceful, and safe. Sit in a comfortable position. You may close your eyes if you wish, or keep them open. Allow your focus to soften into the middle distance. Center your attention on your breath and your physical presence. When your thoughts drift, acknowledge them and return to your inward focus.

Now think of a memory surrounding gaslighting or other emotional abuse. Do not go straight to your most painful memory; choose one that feels moderately painful. Allow the memory to surface, and observe as many details as you can. Spend a few moments exploring this memory.

Begin to take note of the emotions that arise. Choose one that feels strong, and allow your internal gaze to softly focus on that feeling. Name the feeling, saying something like "this is anger," or "this is grief." Try not to judge your feelings.

Next, allow your focus to shift to your physical self. Scan your body from the top of your head to the soles of your feet. Continue to hold awareness of the emotion you identified previously. Ask your body to show you where the emotion is held.

When you find the feeling, place a hand gently on the area where you notice the sensation. Imagine sending a wave of love to that place as you say, "I offer myself compassion for my anger," or, "I offer myself compassion for my grief." Notice how your physical and emotional selves react to your compassion. Do they soften? Resist? Continue to send compassion until you feel a softening. Thank your body for showing you how it holds this emotion. If you'd like, connect with your body in a soothing way by giving yourself a hug, stretching your arms to the ceiling, or massaging your neck.

Self-Talk Exercises

Have you ever noticed the way you talk to yourself *about* yourself? The way we think about and talk to ourselves is called *self-talk*. Self-talk can be kind, compassionate, and positive, or harsh, critical, and negative. What does your self-talk sound like?

Gaslighting can have a negative effect on self-talk and self-perception. In this section, we will explore how your self-talk reflects your beliefs about yourself. The following writing prompts are designed to help you shift negative, critical self-talk toward kindness and self-compassion.

Self-Description Exercise

You can learn a lot about your self-talk by paying close attention to the kinds of words you use to describe yourself *to* yourself. Here, give it a try.

Describe yourself in five words or phrases.

_____

_____

_____

_____

_____

_____

_____

_____

_____

_____

What kinds of words did you choose? Did you describe yourself in positive, negative, or neutral terms? If you focused on what you consider to be negative attributes, then your self-talk is likely negative.

Try the exercise again, this time emphasizing self-compassionate language. For example, instead of describing yourself as "overly emotional," try "attuned to my feelings," or "appropriately sensitive."

Say It to Your Bestie

Pretend you are listening to your best friend talk about a time they were gaslit. Imagine that they tell you they feel stupid for letting themselves be manipulated, and they fear they'll never recover from the abuse. How would you respond to them? Now imagine giving yourself the same kindness. Write your response here.

_____

_____

_____

_____

_____

_____

_____

_____

_____

_____

_____

_____

_____

_____

_____

_____

_____

_____

Emotional Abuse Is Not Gendered

According to the National Domestic Violence Hotline, nearly half of all women and men (48.4% and 48.8%, respectively) experience psychological aggression by a partner during their lifetime. While much of the research and presentation of emotional abuse in the media is presented as men victimizing women, men can also be gaslit by female partners, friends, family members, and colleagues. There is also an additional social stigma for men who have been abused, as being victimized may be seen as weakness. As previously noted, gender nonbinary individuals can also be both victims and perpetrators of emotional abuse. No one is immune.

What You Do Is Not Who You Are

Make a list of personality or character traits with which you identify. Practice separating *who you are* from *what you do*.

I AM MY TRAITS	MY TRAITS ARE . . .
I am too trusting.	Giving people who have not earned it the benefit of the doubt

Self-Compassion Journal

Keep a journal of daily events that offer opportunities to practice self-compassion. For each incident, note the following three aspects:

1. **Provide mindful awareness.** What happened, and how did you feel about it? Try to be non-judgmental and non-critical as you note your emotions.

2. **Normalize your reaction.** Write a line or two about how your response speaks to a common humanity. For example, many people become frustrated when another driver cuts them off in traffic. Being frustrated is a normal response.

3. **Offer self-kindness.** Write a few lines offering yourself compassion, reassurance, and comfort. Try to be kind and gentle.

What happened, and how did I feel about it?

_____

_____

_____

_____

_____

How is my reaction common to humanity?

_____

_____

_____

_____

_____

I can show myself kindness by:

_____

_____

_____

_____

Complete this exercise daily for at least one week, and see how you feel at the end of the week.

Letter of Self-Forgiveness

Many survivors of abuse struggle with self-blame. They feel they could have prevented the abuse by behaving differently, ending the relationship sooner, or leaving and not coming back. Do you blame yourself for anything related to your abuse? If so, write yourself a kind letter offering yourself forgiveness. Be specific about what you forgive yourself for, and avoid placing conditions on your forgiveness.

_____

_____

_____

_____

_____

_____

_____

_____

_____

_____

_____

_____

_____

_____

_____

_____

_____

_____

_____

_____

_____

_____

_____

Internalized Gaslighting

If you are having difficulty showing yourself kindness and compassion, explore the reasons behind your hesitation. Take note if your self-talk includes messages like "You deserve to be gaslit because you were too stupid to see what was happening," or, "Well, he was right, you are a lazy slob. If you just cleaned up once in a while, he wouldn't have any reason to say that."

These messages are an indication of *internalized gaslighting*, which can happen when you have become so accustomed to emotional abuse you turn harsh words and sentiments on yourself, sometimes as a form of self-protection. Gaslighting yourself might make you less likely to show the kind of confidence and assertiveness that deters further abuse from the other person in your relationship. Internalized gaslighting is also a way that abuse can continue even when an abuser is not physically present. If you recognize yourself in this way of thinking, the next exercise will be especially valuable.

Affirmations

Practice counteracting negative self-messages with affirmations. Notice if this task is difficult, and ask yourself what feels bad or wrong. I encourage you to persevere, even if you find this exercise hard. Believing that you are worthy of treating yourself with love and compassion is a mind-set that must be learned and practiced.

Here are some examples of affirmations that promote self-compassion:

"I deserve to be treated with respect."

"I do not deserve to be manipulated and emotionally abused."

"I have compassion for the parts of me that have been hurt by abusive relationships."

"I accept the part of myself that wants to believe the best in people and may excuse hurtful behavior."

"I am worthy of love and compassion."

Create five affirmations of your own below. Say them to yourself daily!

_____

_____

_____

_____

_____

_____

_____

_____

_____

_____

_____

_____

_____

_____

_____

_____

_____

_____

_____

_____

_____

_____

Self-Compassion Daily Log

For one week, keep a daily log of how you treat yourself throughout the day.

Read each question carefully before responding. For each day, rate how often you felt compassionate or critical. (Adapted from ACT compassion self-rating.)

Hardly Ever		**Almost Always**		**Always**
1	**2**	**3**	**4**	**5**

	MON	TUES	WEDS	THURS	FRI	SAT	SUN
When I had problems today, I saw my difficulties as a normal part of life that everyone goes through.							
When I felt emotional pain today, I tried to be loving toward myself.							
When I felt upset or unhappy today, I tried to remind myself that other people feel this way, too.							
When I had problems today, I was very hard on myself.							
I was gentle and kind toward myself today.							
I saw my mistakes as normal and human today.							
I was loving and nurturing to the parts of me that were hurting today.							
I was harsh, distant, and unloving toward myself today.							
When something hurt me today, I tried to be openhearted and curious toward myself.							
I was unforgiving of my human flaws today.							
I was impatient and judgmental toward the parts of me I don't care for.							

Visualize a Compassionate Future

In this exercise, you will create a vision board to represent your journey toward self-compassion.

On one side, the collage will have pictures, words, interesting textures, and other materials that represent a relationship characterized by gaslighting. The relationship can take place in any context (familial, personal, professional, romantic, etc.). The words and images you choose should illustrate the confusion, lack of self-confidence, anxiety, and other side effects you experienced in that relationship.

On the other side, you can represent your post-gaslighting self. This board should illustrate your awareness and self-compassion. Create an image that speaks to your commitment to recover from abuse. If you are still struggling to let go of the gaslighter's influence, think of your second side as aspirational. How do you *want* to see yourself?

Put your vision board in a visible place so you can get regular reminders of how far you've come!

Give It Away

On a scrap of paper, write down a word, phrase, memory, or image associated with your gaslighting experiences. Read your message, then fold the paper up as small as you can. Dispose of the paper by releasing it to one of the elements—bury it in the earth, shred it and throw it to the wind, float it out to sea, or burn it (safely!). As you release the words, say to yourself "I do not need to carry this gaslighting with me anymore."

Manifest Self-Compassion

You may find yourself still struggling to shake off your gaslighter's criticisms and character assaults. If you find self-compassion hard to manage, that's okay. Start by speaking your intention to become kinder to yourself. When you put your intentions out to the universe, you're enabling your intentions to come to life within you.

Write a statement manifesting loving-kindness for yourself. Phrase your statement as a current action—even if you're struggling to connect with the loving-kindness.

Example: "I make space in my heart for self-compassion. I welcome kindness from myself and to myself."

_____

_____

_____

_____

_____

Review and Wrap-Up

Look back at the exercises in this chapter.

What resonated with you the most?

_____

_____

_____

_____

_____

_____

What did not resonate?

_____

_____

_____

How do you feel right now? How have your feelings changed since you started this chapter?

_____

_____

_____

_____

_____

_____

_____

_____

What will you take away from these exercises?

_____

_____

_____

_____

_____

_____

_____

_____

Phase Two (Building Self-Esteem)

Welcome to phase two in your recovery—where you begin to heal the damage done to your self-esteem. In the first two chapters, we covered what gaslighting looks like and the effects of this form of abuse on victims. In chapter 3, we explored the signs and side effects of gaslighting for you, personally, and began developing self-compassion. Now we will continue your recovery journey by rebuilding your self-esteem and developing assertiveness.

Chapter 4 has exercises and journal prompts intended to help you identify the damage to your self-esteem from toxic relationships and learn ways to rebuild your self-confidence and assert yourself in relationships. Part of your recovery involves understanding and practicing different styles of communication and ways to appreciate yourself more and bolstering a mind-set of growth and gratitude.

Some of these exercises will feel hard. It can be difficult to think positively about yourself after having been gaslit into believing you were no more than your flaws. Be patient with yourself. Gaslighting would not be as effective at controlling people without the lingering effects. Take your time, and be kind to the parts of yourself that struggle with these exercises.

Let's begin!

Assertive Bill of Rights

Many survivors of emotional abuse struggle with asserting themselves in relationships. They have been conditioned to perceive speaking up for themselves as a sign of selfishness. **That is a lie**.

The following is an Assertive Bill of Rights, adapted from Manuel J. Smith's "A Bill of Assertive Rights" (1975). Read through each of the following items, and note how you feel:

I have the right to judge my own thoughts, feelings, and behaviors, independent of anyone else's assessment of them.

I have the right to my thoughts and feelings without needing to justify or apologize for them.

I have the right to determine whether I share responsibility for finding solutions to someone else's problems, and to act accordingly.

I have the right to change my mind.

I have the right to say "no" without feeling guilty.

I have the right to make mistakes, and the responsibility to address them when they occur.

I have the right to say "I don't know."

I have the right to say "I don't care."

I have the right to take up physical, mental, and emotional space.

I have the right to feel compassion for someone without being responsible for fixing them.

I have the right to make the best choice for me, even if this choice is not what someone else would prefer.

I have the right to form my own set of values, moral code, and ethics independent of others.

I have the right to disengage or choose not to engage with persons who are hurtful to me.

I have the right to walk away from a toxic relationship, no matter what kind.

I have the right to be my own person, with all the unique and special individualities that make me different from every other person in the world.

Writing Exercise

How did you feel as you read each line of the Assertive Bill of Rights? What resonated and what did not? Did any of the rights feel particularly hard to accept or agree with? Write your response(s) to the Assertive Bill of Rights here.

_____

_____

_____

_____

_____

_____

_____

_____

_____

_____

_____

_____

_____

_____

_____

_____

_____

_____

_____

_____

Pay special attention to the rights that were hardest to accept. Those will touch on places most in need of healing.

Self-esteem refers to your personal sense of worth and value. Your level of self-esteem has a significant and direct impact on how you carry yourself in relationships and how you expect to be treated. If your self-esteem is too low, you believe you don't deserve to be treated with love and respect. You automatically assume others are above you. You are more likely to accept abuse because you don't believe you're worthy of anything better.

If your self-esteem is too high, you may be grandiose, arrogant, and have unrealistic expectations of being seen as exceptional. You may believe yourself to be above others. Excessive self-esteem can be part of a narcissistic personality. The sad irony is that some narcissists actually feel deeply unworthy, and their grandiosity, gaslighting, and social climbing are largely part of an attempt to feel more valuable.

With healthy self-esteem, you can appreciate your strengths, acknowledge your flaws, and take responsibility for your mistakes without believing they negatively impact your value as a person. You can expect fair treatment in relationships and feel empowered to walk away from toxic or abusive behavior. You *can* teach people how to treat you—and that begins with how you treat yourself.

REPAIRING THE DAMAGE

Emotional abusers create victims by chipping away at their self-esteem over time. Fortunately, what was chipped away can be rebuilt. The following exercise will take you through three steps to understand the ways your self-esteem was damaged and teach you ways to begin healing.

Step one: Write down or draw a picture showing a word, phrase, or behavior that was used to gaslight you.

Step two: Write down or draw a picture showing how this word, phrase, or behavior from step 1 made you think and feel about yourself.

Step three: Write or draw a picture of an alternative belief about yourself to counteract the gaslighter's message. Now say this belief out loud. Notice how you feel about yourself as you speak your new message.

GASLIGHTING MESSAGE ABOUT MY VALUE	HOW THE GASLIGHTING MESSAGE MADE ME FEEL ABOUT MYSELF	ALTERNATIVE MESSAGE ABOUT MY VALUE
Example: "You'd be so pretty if you lost weight."	I am ugly because I'm fat. No one will want me unless I lose weight.	My value is not contingent on being a certain weight. I am worthy of love at any size.

Best Friend Bio

Imagine that your best friend has been asked to contribute to your biography. He or she will be asked details of who you are as a person and what makes you special. The biography will focus on your unique personality traits, personal accomplishments, skills, and strengths. Write at least one paragraph about yourself through your best friend's eyes. The following questions are suggested prompts, but be creative! The only requirement is that you focus on the positive qualities that your best friend celebrates.

Suggested interview prompts:

What would your best friend say makes you special?

What strengths and skills do you possess?

What about you is your best friend most proud of?

What does your best friend appreciate most about you?

_____

_____

_____

_____

_____

Bonus Option

Sit down with your best friend and use these questions to conduct an actual interview. Write your friend's responses here.

_____

_____

_____

_____

_____

_____

_____

Strengths Survey

We all have unique strengths, skills, and personality traits that make us special. If you haven't thought about the qualities that make you *you* in a while, now is your chance: In this exercise, outline everything that is great about you.

Think about the things you like most about yourself, whether intrinsic personality traits or skills you've developed over your lifetime. This is not the time to be humble. This is the time to name and take pride in everything that makes you special!

As you write about your strengths, skills, and special traits, think about how you've developed them over your lifetime. How might you develop them further throughout the rest of your life?

One aspect I like about myself is:

_____

_____

_____

_____

_____

One aspect I am good at is:

_____

_____

_____

_____

_____

_____

One aspect that is unique about me is:

_____

_____

_____

_____

_____

The strength, skill, or trait I am most proud of myself for is:

_____

_____

_____

_____

_____

I discovered this strength/skill/trait by:

_____

_____

_____

_____

_____

A superpower based on my actual strengths, skills, and traits would be:

_____

_____

_____

_____

_____

I would use this superpower in this way:

_____

_____

_____

_____

_____

The "I Love You" Exercise

During the last exercise, you may have noticed your inner critic having some things to say about your strengths, skills, and personality traits. If you find saying anything nice about yourself hard, this next exercise is especially for you. You might hate it—do it anyway.

Inner critics are the parts of us that have internalized the harsh and critical messages we received in abusive relationships. What we sometimes think of as "being a perfectionist" is simply an inner critic doing everything to prevent you from making mistakes. The inner critic is hard on you, not out of hate, but out of an attempt to help you avoid becoming the target of further abuse. Your inner critic is trying to protect you by making you so aware of your flaws you hyper-compensate for them. In other words, behind the harsh approach is a good intention.

This exercise is all about bringing love to yourself, flaws and all. Self-esteem starts with one word: self. To feel good about yourself, you must be loving toward yourself. And that love extends even to the parts of you that can be critical of you. This exercise will help you find your love.

"I Love You" Meditation

Close your eyes and imagine sitting across the table from your inner critic. Picture yourself sitting or standing close enough to your inner critic to see its eyes and hear its voice. Notice if you feel anxious, sad, angry, or afraid. Breathe deeply and slowly, using your diaphragm and feeling your belly expand with each inhalation and deflate with each exhalation. Breathe in peace, calm, and confidence; breathe out fear, anger, and anxiety. Look at your critic and tell it you are here to have a talk.

Begin by telling the critic you'll listen to what it has to say now, and that you are ready to hear what it doesn't like about you. Ask the critic to name one complaint at a time so that you can hear the criticism and respond. Make sure to check in with your breathing throughout the meditation. Continue to breathe slowly and deeply, feeling your breath filling and emptying your lungs.

As you listen to your inner critic, try to remain curious and open. Do you recognize the voice? How do you feel when you hear something negative about you? Where do you feel the response, in or around your body? If you feel worried, upset, or distracted, return to your deep breathing until you can resume your conversation with the inner critic.

This Is Important

Every time your inner critic names a complaint, pause. Notice how you feel and where you feel that response. Place a hand on the place where you feel your emotional response, and say, "I love you."

Repeat this step after every criticism.

How do you feel as you say "I love you" after every criticism? Does your heart feel hard, constricted, or wounded? Place a hand over your heart and say, "I love you."

Continue repeating "I love you" until you feel your heart soften, warm, and open up full of love. When you feel your heart is open and full of love, look at your inner critic—that part of you that reminds you of every mistake and flaw—and say, "I love you, too." How does the critic respond?

Continue sending love to the parts hurt by the criticism you have internalized. Send love to your inner critic—the part of you that has remembered these messages—so that you'll never be hurt again. Feel the love in your heart. It's enough to cover every wound you've received.

Breathe in love, breathe out pain. Place a hand over your heart and say, "I love you."

The I Love You Meditation can stir up many feelings. What did you notice as you completed the meditation? Write your response to the exercise here:

_____

_____

_____

_____

_____

Positive Traits Experienced

For the traits listed below, write about a time you embodied each. How have your positive traits been helpful for you and others?

Courage:

_____

_____

_____

_____

Kindness:

_____

_____

_____

_____

Generosity:

_____

_____

_____

_____

Love:

_____

_____

_____

_____

Mercy:

_____

_____

_____

_____

Wisdom:

_____

_____

_____

_____

Hopefulness:

_____

_____

_____

_____

Joy:

_____

_____

_____

_____

Determination:

_____

_____

_____

_____

Patience:

_____

_____

_____

_____

Perseverance:

_____

_____

_____

_____

Intuition:

_____

_____

_____

_____

_____

What's Wrong with You vs. What Happened to You

The way you talk to yourself can be a powerful force for self-compassion or for self-gaslighting, greatly influencing your sense of personal worth and value. When you feel badly about yourself, you'll likely find it much harder to engage in assertive communication.

This exercise builds on the compassionate "Self-Talk Exercises" you practiced in chapter 3 (see page 39). Begin by writing out a statement you might currently use to describe yourself based on your experiences. Then, rewrite that statement as an event or situation that affected you, but does not define you.

WHAT'S WRONG WITH ME	WHAT HAPPENED TO ME
I am damaged goods.	I have been hurt by an abusive relationship.

History of Growth Timeline

Sometimes when we become overly focused on our flaws and mistakes, we lose sight of the progress we've made. This exercise helps track your growth in one or more areas of your life. You may map your progress in a mental, emotional, spiritual, or physical skill, or in a specific aspect of abuse recovery such as regaining confidence or building up resilience.

On the following page, create a timeline showing your growth and progress in one or more areas. Track your progress over the last week, month, year, five years, ten years, or more. How has this strength changed as you have grown? How far have you come?

You may also wish to note times you stumbled, got lost, got stuck, or backtracked in your progress. All a normal part of growth! Be proud of yourself for growing through the challenges.

Taking the Next Step

After completing your timeline, you may consider creating a new set of goals to pursue. Is there a particular skill, interest, or strength you would like to cultivate? An aspect of healing and recovery that merits a more focused approach?

Consider today to be the first step of your next timeline of growth. Where do you want to grow from here? Identify three to five goals that you can work toward as you move forward in your life. Where do you want to be in a year? Five years? Ten? Think boldly! The sky is the limit.

_____

_____

_____

_____

_____

_____

_____

_____

History of Growth Timeline

TIMELINE TITLE:

Daily Appreciation

As soon as you wake up, write down at least one thing you appreciate about yourself. Take your note, stand in front of a mirror, and read the message out loud to yourself at least three times. Look at yourself in the mirror as you speak and don't worry about sounding silly. Place the note in a safe place, and review the message again at the end of the day.

Repeat this exercise every day for 100 days, appreciating something different about yourself each time. Put a reminder in your calendar or set an alarm on your phone to help you remember to spend a few moments every day in appreciation. Keep your notes and put them into a scrapbook or make a collage with them at the end of this period.

Daily Gratitude

In a similar vein to the "Daily Appreciation" exercise, end your day by writing down at least one thing for which you are grateful. What you choose can be large or small, significant or trivial. Prepare yourself for sleep by spending five minutes focusing on something for which you feel thankful.

With Abundance: Manifesting Self-Esteem

Create five affirmations or mantras to welcome in and make space for healthy self-esteem and self-respect. On the following page, write each affirmation as if you've already received these gifts of self. Offer gratitude to the universe, or whatever resonates for you spiritually, for your health and healing.

Examples:

"I love and appreciate myself exactly as I am."

"I welcome self-respect and healthy self-confidence."

"I give thanks for the wisdom and resilience of my heart."

Your turn:

_____

_____

_____

_____

_____

Claim Your Space

Body language can reveal a lot about us. How we sit, stand, and move can reflect our level of comfort with taking up space in the world. This exercise helps you explore what your body language says about your self-esteem. You will need enough room to stretch out, so find an open area where you can stand. If you can be in front of a mirror, that's great, but it's okay if you can't. If you're unable to stand, sit up as straight and tall as possible.

Think of a time when you felt small, ashamed, unworthy, or unhappy with yourself. What does your body look and feel like when you don't value yourself very highly? Do you sit or stand tall? Slump? Are you looking down? Hunching your shoulders? Take about a minute to focus on your body language when you don't feel good about yourself.

Now imagine yourself as confident, assertive, and aware of your value. You love yourself and own your right to take up space in the world. Let's practice claiming your physical space as a confident, assertive, worthy person.

Stand with your feet at least hip-width apart, arms hanging loosely by your sides. If you cannot stand, sit up tall with your back as straight as possible. Feel your feet firmly in contact with the floor. Your weight should be spread evenly between your big toes, pinkie toes, and heels (or firmly on both sit bones if you are seated). Press your feet into the floor and imagine lifting up through your torso at the same time. Sit or stand comfortably straight. Feel tall, strong through your core, and balanced.

Slightly contract the muscles of your legs, buttocks, and upper back. Don't clench; your goal is simply to become aware of the strength your body possesses. Feel the energy in your muscles.

Gently pull your shoulder blades back and down. Feel the open space in your chest and across your collarbones. Raise your arms to the side, either at a low diagonal, shoulder height, or high diagonal, whichever feels best to you. Raise your chin and look up on a high diagonal. Feel energy shooting down your arms and out of your fingertips. Feel the space around your heart expand. *Claim your space.*

Raise your arms straight overhead and press your palms together. Lift your face and gaze at the sky. Feel your feet grounded on the floor as you reach upward and make yourself tall. *Claim your space.*

Bring your arms to chest level, keeping your palms together and lowering your gaze to look straight ahead. Pull your elbows back and place your hands on your hips, feeling your shoulder blades pulling down and back again. Lift your chest slightly, feeling energy through your shoulders, upper arms, and hands or fists as they rest on your hips. Feel your solid physical presence. *Claim your space.*

As you finish this exercise and relax your stance, try to hold on to the openness around your heart. Reflect on how you feel now compared to how you felt at the beginning of the exercise.

Defining Assertiveness

Assertive communication and an assertive mind-set are often the ideals. Yet finding the happy medium between being a doormat and being a steamroller can be surprisingly hard. For recovering passives, many of the barriers to assertiveness lie in their own beliefs about what advocating for self means. In this exercise, we will explore your thoughts and beliefs about your own assertiveness.

What does assertiveness mean to you?

_____

_____

_____

Identify someone in your life you think of as assertive. How do they act? How do you feel around them?

_____

_____

_____

_____

What benefits do you see to becoming more assertive yourself? What drawbacks might there be?

_____

_____

_____

_____

When you imagine yourself speaking assertively, what are the "buts" in your self-talk? What feels scary, risky, or unnerving about asserting yourself?

_____

_____

_____

_____

How might your life change if you became more assertive? Do you think things would change for the better, or for the worse? What are the risks and rewards of changing?

_____

_____

_____

_____

THE BENEFITS OF ASSERTIVENESS

While developing assertiveness can be difficult for gaslighting victims, the potential payoff is significant. Assertive communication has many benefits, including:

* Increased confidence and self-esteem
* Decreased stress
* Greater ability to recognize and understand your feelings
* More respect from others
* Better communication skills
* More honest relationships
* Positive change
* Increased sense of self-efficacy

When you get tired and start to question why you're working so hard to become more assertive, write down the ways these benefits could improve your life.

_____

_____

_____

_____

_____

_____

_____

_____

_____

_____

_____

_____

_____

_____

_____

_____

_____

_____

Communication Styles

Most communication falls into one of four general categories or styles: Passive, Aggressive, Passive-Aggressive, and Assertive. How we communicate can have a significant impact on how we are perceived by others, and how we conduct ourselves in relationships.

Passive communication is timid, self-effacing, withdrawn, avoidant, and lacks confidence. Passivity may also show up as being a people-pleaser or feeling like a doormat in relationships. Many emotional abuse victims are passive communicators.

Aggressive communication is forceful, direct, blunt, and controlling. Verbal aggression may include honesty without empathy, or "brutal honesty," which is hurtful without being constructive. Aggressive communicators are not always, but can be, emotionally domineering and abusive.

Passive-aggressive communication is indirect, manipulative, covert, and emotionally dishonest. A passive-aggressive communicator may report one feeling, but show something different through their behaviors and attitudes. Passive-aggressive communication can cause confusion, guilt, and frustration in recipients, as well as provoke resentment and a martyr complex in speakers. Individuals with narcissistic or borderline traits are often passive-aggressive communicators.

Assertive communication is honest, direct, thoughtful, and confident. Assertive communicators are open and firm, solidly grounded in their right to express themselves responsibly. Assertive communicators temper their honesty with empathy. They are willing to compromise when appropriate, and trust their judgment against manipulation.

Chart: Find Your Communication Style

Assertiveness is not just a communication style, but a way of life. Assertive communication is just one aspect of embodying your right to be treated with humanity and respect. That said, how you communicate can have a significant impact on how people perceive and respond to you.

The chart below outlines four different communication styles. Which one is most like you?

PASSIVE	AGGRESSIVE
Emotionally dishonest (withholding one's own feelings)	Inappropriately honest ("brutal" honesty with no regard for the feelings of others)
Indirect (hinting, insinuating)	Self-promoting at the expense of others
Self-denying	Attacking
Timid, self-effacing	Blaming and shaming
Blaming	Controlling
Resentful	Threatening
Apologetic	Overriding others' sense of self for personal gain
Withholding true self for fear of loss	"I have to always win."
"I always lose."	

PASSIVE-AGGRESSIVE	ASSERTIVE
Emotionally dishonest (words and behaviors do not match up)	Appropriately honest
Indirect and avoidant	Firm and direct
Denying of self, followed by self-promotion	Respecting of oneself and the other person
Inflicting guilt trips to achieve compliance	Empathetic of others' positions
Self-promoting at the expense of others	Openly expressive of thoughts, feelings, and needs
Possibly accusatory	Confident without being arrogant
Temporarily withholding true self out of fear or obligation	Willing to compromise appropriately
"No one lets me win, and it's their fault."	Showing concern for both parties' well-being
	"We don't have to compete."

Writing Exercise

Choose a scenario that upsets you. Write out at least one sentence responding to the incident in each of the four communication styles. Be creative! Try out different styles, and pay attention to how you feel practicing in a low-risk way.

Example: Your brother borrows your car without asking and brings it back with no gas in the tank and a dent in one fender. How could you address this situation with him?

PASSIVE	AGGRESSIVE
PASSIVE-AGGRESSIVE	ASSERTIVE

I-Statements

A key aspect of assertiveness is knowing you have the right to express your wants and needs. Sometimes victims of emotional abuse struggle with being direct in naming how they feel and asking for what they want. Here, you will practice using clear, direct I-statements to express your wants and needs. Remember: Asking is not demanding. Expressing your needs is not selfish.

Exercise:

Write out an indirect request or expression you might normally use. Then rewrite that expression using a direct I-statement.

Examples:

Indirect Expression: "It would really be nice if you could be a little nicer to me."

I-Statement: "I would like you to speak more kindly," or, "I don't like it when you call me names."

Indirect Expression: "When you make fun of my feelings, it kind of feels like you think I'm silly for having them."

I-Statement: "I am entitled to my feelings. You may not agree with them, but I need you to respect them."

Indirect Expression:

_____

_____

_____

_____

_____

I-Statement:

_____

_____

_____

_____

_____

Indirect Expression:

_____

_____

_____

_____

_____

I-Statement:

_____

_____

_____

_____

_____

Indirect Expression:

_____

_____

_____

_____

_____

I-Statement:

_____

_____

_____

_____

_____

Indirect Expression:

_____

_____

_____

_____

_____

I-Statement:

_____

_____

_____

_____

_____

Indirect Expression:

_____

_____

_____

_____

_____

I-Statement:

_____

_____

_____

_____

_____

Barriers to Assertiveness

Have you ever wondered why you can be assertive in some situations, but others leave you tongue-tied and confused? Maybe you can speak up on behalf of your child, but advocating for yourself gives you hives. Or you can march right up to someone mistreating an animal and tell them off, but asking your boss to approve your vacation time makes your knees shake. What is the difference between the times you can be assertive and when you can't?

Sometimes we hold unconscious beliefs about ourselves that influence our behaviors in subtle ways. This exercise helps identify any unconscious beliefs you may have and examine how these beliefs may affect your ability to assert yourself.

Write about a time you were assertive.

_____

_____

_____

_____

_____

What kinds of thoughts and feelings did you have at that time?

_____

_____

_____

_____

_____

What made you decide to speak or act in that situation?

_____

_____

_____

_____

_____

Now think about a time you wanted to be assertive but couldn't. What happened?

_____

_____

_____

_____

_____

What kinds of thoughts and feelings did you have at that time?

_____

_____

_____

_____

_____

What made you decide not to assert yourself at that time?

_____

_____

_____

_____

_____

What is different about these two scenarios? How did you talk to yourself in each scenario?

_____

_____

_____

_____

_____

De-nice-ify Yourself

Raise your hand if your previous attempts to assert yourself were ever met with some variation of "That's not very nice." Niceness has been used—to great effect—to suppress and control personal expression by strictly defining how and when expressing a need is acceptable. People of all genders can be subject to strong societal messages about niceness. Women are the target of social expectations to be nice, charming, agreeable, empathetic, flexible, and accommodating. Men are taught that niceness is currency for women's sexual engagement. In addition to gender expectations, minority populations are often unfairly burdened by an expectation to be nice when confronting oppression or abuse, lest their advocacy be considered "too aggressive."

In these cases, the individuals are taught to present a false face—one that disguises their true feelings beneath a patina of "niceness." In neither case can the individuals be fully genuine and truthful. Niceness comes at the expense of honesty and authenticity. That is not to say that the only way to be authentic is to act like a jerk. It is to say, though, that it is possible to be kind, compassionate, honest, and truthful without putting the "need" to be "nice" above your own needs.

What messages have you received about being nice? Write down what you've been taught.

Example: If I call out a sexist joke at work, people will think I'm a "killjoy" and a "feminazi." I should just learn to let these situations go. (*I should be quiet and agreeable—aka, "nice."*)

_____

_____

_____

_____

_____

Now write a counter to each of these messages.

_____

_____

_____

_____

_____

Example: If I call out a sexist joke at work, I am setting a boundary and expressing my opinion. My thoughts and feelings are valid. (*I do not need to suppress my opinion to appease a disrespectful coworker*).

_____

_____

_____

_____

_____

Fears of a People-Pleaser

Passive people often fear that self-advocacy will come off as selfish or aggressive. A people-pleaser's greatest fear is to upset someone else. But what makes that fear so intense? What would be so bad about upsetting someone?

With this exercise, you explore underlying fears that influence your need to people-please. This exercise is adapted from techniques used in a therapeutic model called Internal Family Systems. As you work through this exercise, you will see a question repeated several times. Do your best to approach the question each time as an honest, non-sarcastic, non-rhetorical inquiry. Channel the self-compassion you developed in chapter 3 as you interact with the fearful parts of yourself.

Begin by remembering a time you wanted to assert yourself but did not out of fear of upsetting someone. Think about how you felt in that moment. What did you worry or fear would happen if you upset the person?

I was worried/afraid that:

_____

_____

_____

_____

_____

Listen for the fear. Perhaps part of you is afraid that if you do not people-please by, say, doing your mother's bidding, she will become angry with you. Now, with openhearted curiosity, ask yourself, "And what would be bad for me if that happened?"

What would be the worst part of the response you've given?

_____

_____

_____

_____

_____

_____

Listen again for the fear. Perhaps this part is afraid that if your mother is angry at you, she will think you are a bad son. With openhearted curiosity ask yourself, "And what would be bad for me if that happened?"

_____

_____

_____

_____

_____

What would be the worst part of the response you've given?

_____

_____

_____

_____

Listen again. Perhaps this part of you fears that if your mother thinks you are a bad son, you truly _will be_ a bad son. And that would be bad because the worst part of being a bad son is that she might not love you anymore.

Be kind, compassionate, and patient with the parts of you afraid to rock the boat. Several repetitions of that openhearted question, "What would be the worst part?" may be needed to get to the deep fear that drives your people-pleasing behavior. Continue to offer self-compassion to your fearful parts, and remind them that you can love and care for yourself no matter what anyone else does.

Reflective Listening

Reflective listening refers to another aspect of assertive communication: hearing the other person's concerns. To practice reflective listening, listen carefully to what the other person is saying. Then, at your turn to speak, calmly repeat back what you heard. Use the other person's exact words to show your understanding of their thoughts or feelings. This kind of listening shows the other person you are paying attention, and you take them seriously.

Rinse and Repeat

When you experience gaslighting, over-explaining yourself and trying to convince the gaslighter that your feelings, thoughts, or memories are accurate may be tempting. These tactics are usually futile, however, because the point of gaslighting is to convince you that you are wrong. Sometimes the most effective strategy is to come up with a short phrase you can return to over and over as needed—the *rinse and repeat.*

Rinse and repeat phrases should: 1) acknowledge the other person's position, and 2) reiterate your response.

Example:

Juan: "You need to stay home with the kids tonight so I can go watch the game at Bill's."

Esme: "I know you want me to stay home tonight, but I already have plans so you will need to find a babysitter."

Juan: "You are being selfish. What kind of mother won't take care of her own kids?"

Esme: "I know you want me to stay home tonight, but I already have plans so you will need to find a babysitter."

Juan: "I can't believe you. What is the matter with you? How can you be so cold to your own family?"

Esme: "I understand that you're upset, but I already made plans and I am not canceling them. You will need to find a babysitter. I am heading out now. I'll text when I'm on my way home."

Create at least three rinse and repeat phrases to assertively stand your ground:

Rinse and Repeat #1:

_____

_____

_____

_____

_____

Rinse and Repeat #2:

_____

_____

_____

_____

_____

Rinse and Repeat #3:

_____

_____

_____

_____

_____

Find a Workable Compromise

Being assertive does not mean insisting on getting your way all the time. Assertive communication involves taking into account and respecting the needs and concerns of all parties. Sometimes the appropriate result is finding a workable compromise between two opposing needs. To find a workable compromise, use reflective listening to identify the conflicting needs. Then, create a counter-offer you believe affords equal consideration to your needs as well as to the needs of the other person.

Note: When you are in an abusive situation and your abuser is trying to steamroll you, you may need to be more firm in advocating for your needs. Finding a truly workable compromise presupposes at least minimal mutual respect in a relationship.

This exercise helps you practice offering a workable compromise that does not make you feel steamrolled while acknowledging the needs of the other person.

Examples:

"I hear that you really want to talk to me about this situation, but I need to finish what I am working on right now. How about we check in 15 minutes from now, when I can give you my full attention?"

"I am not able to dog-sit for you this weekend, but here is the website of a friend of mine who runs a dog-sitting business."

"I'm sorry, but I can't loan you money again this month. If you would like, I could sit down with you next week and have a look at your budget. Maybe I can help you find a way to stretch your dollars a little further."

The Request:

_____

_____

_____

_____

_____

Your Workable Compromise:

_____

_____

_____

_____

_____

The Request:

_____

_____

_____

_____

_____

Your Workable Compromise:

_____

_____

_____

_____

_____

The Request:

_____

_____

_____

_____

_____

Your Workable Compromise:

_____

_____

_____

_____

_____

Review and Wrap-Up

Look back at the exercises in this chapter.

What resonated with you the most?

_____

_____

_____

_____

_____

_____

What did not resonate?

_____

_____

_____

_____

_____

_____

How do you feel right now? Have your feelings changed since you started this chapter?

_____

_____

_____

_____

_____

_____

What will you take away from these exercises?

_____

_____

_____

_____

_____

_____

CHAPTER 5

Phase Three (Establishing Boundaries)

Welcome to phase three in your gaslighting recovery. This chapter addresses ways to establish boundaries in current and future relationships. Learning this skill is a crucial aspect of your recovery, because strong, healthy boundaries are necessary for relationships to grow and flourish.

This chapter's exercises and writing prompts are designed to help you identify and establish boundaries that work for you. Beginning with an exploration of what boundaries are and what they mean to you, the chapter moves into identifying your personal values and boundaries and learning how to say "no" without guilt.

You may find the idea of establishing boundaries scary or uncomfortable. Feeling this way is normal. You have probably worked hard to avoid antagonizing or upsetting your abuser as much as possible. Defying the will of a controlling person can be a surefire way to upset them. Establishing boundaries does not guarantee that an abuser's behavior will change for the better. But the boundaries do help you determine what you will and will not tolerate, how you will and will not participate in relationships, and where your walk-away lines are. Boundaries are *empowerment*.

Let's begin.

Boundaries are what separates one person, place, or thing from another. You can learn to manage your boundaries in many different areas, including material property, physical space/involvement, mental and emotional engagement, sexual activity, socialization, and time.

FACT FROM FICTION: SEPARATING MYTHS AND TRUTHS ABOUT BOUNDARIES

What are the facts and fictions about boundaries? You may have heard many messages about how boundaries work and whether they are good. Here, we will dispel some of the myths you may have encountered, and replace them with facts.

Myth: Establishing boundaries will make someone else change their problematic behavior.

There is a common misconception that boundaries are a way to change someone else's behavior. While that's understandable, establishing boundaries is about you, not the other person.

Fact: Establishing boundaries defines your actions and choices.

You cannot control another person's behavior. Establishing boundaries with the intention of controlling someone else's actions will often lead to disappointment. The other person's reaction is not under your control. Your behavior and choices are.

Myth: Establishing boundaries means I'm putting up walls to keep people out.

In an enmeshed or abusive relationship, attempts to establish boundaries may be wrongly portrayed as rejection.

Fact: Boundaries are more like a picket fence, with a gate you can open or close as needed.

Establishing healthy boundaries is not a rejection, but a thoughtful choice to connect with another person. You may choose to relax your boundaries for individuals who demonstrate respect, care, empathy, and love for you.

Myth: Establishing boundaries is cruel, hurtful, and mean. You should never say "no" to someone you love.

Gaslighters may use a false accusation of meanness to guilt-trip you into giving them their way. One method of guilt-tripping is to insinuate, imply, or outright claim that denying them in any way is an unloving act.

Fact: Establishing boundaries teaches others how to be in a loving relationship with you and allows you to be your best self in your relationships.

Loving relationships do not involve coercing and pressuring each other. When you set boundaries and assert yourself, you show the other person you respect and care for yourself—and that you expect the same from them. And when you love yourself enough to expect compassionate, respectful treatment in relationships, you will shine.

What myths do you believe about boundaries? Write out the myths you have believed, followed by a fact to counter them.

Myth:

_____

_____

Fact:

_____

_____

Myth:

_____

_____

Fact:

_____

_____

Myth:

_____

_____

Fact:

_____

_____

Values Assessment Exercise

Boundaries are the lines between two things, but what establishes those lines? In terms of relationship boundaries, you establish the lines by getting clear about your personal values. Defining your values tells you what is and is not okay with you. Boundaries in relationships have a dual essence—where you end and the other person begins, and what is and is not acceptable for you in relationships. This exercise provides an opportunity to examine each type of relationship boundary and articulate your values for each area.

Material Boundaries

Material boundaries have to do with your possessions—phones, clothing, money, shoes, cars, electronic devices, etc. You may have boundaries around what material property you lend and for how long, how your possessions are used and treated, and how to handle misuse. Material boundaries may be challenged in relationships where you are expected to give free access to your personal property.

Assessing Your Values:

Are you comfortable loaning out or giving away your material possessions? Yes, no, or under what conditions?

_____

_____

_____

_____

Are there things you don't want to share, loan out, or have lost? How do you feel about saying no?

_____

_____

_____

_____

How do you want to express your values around material possessions?

_____

_____

_____

Physical Boundaries

Physical boundaries have to do with your body, personal space, and privacy. How do you feel about people being in your physical space, and how do you protect it? Physical boundaries may be challenged in relationships where people do not respect your need for personal space or privacy, or where you have not been allowed to decline physical contact.

Assessing Your Values:

What level of physical contact are you comfortable with among friends? Coworkers? Family? Romantic partners? What level of physical contact feels unacceptable in any of these relationships?

_____

_____

_____

_____

_____

_____

What are your values around privacy? Do you prefer people to leave the room before you change clothes? Breastfeed your baby? Are you okay with someone talking to you through the door while you're using the restroom?

_____

_____

_____

_____

_____

How do you want to express your values around privacy?

_____

_____

_____

_____

_____

Mental and Emotional Boundaries

Mental boundaries refer to having your own thoughts and opinions, separate from how someone else may think. Emotional boundaries refer to your feelings and emotional responses to events. These boundaries may be challenged in relationships where you are expected to think and feel like everyone else, and independence is not valued.

Assessing Your Values:

How important is forming your own thoughts and opinions, even if these differ from the thoughts and opinions of those around you?

_____

_____

_____

_____

_____

_____

How important is having your own feelings, even if your emotional experiences differ from those around you?

_____

_____

_____

_____

_____

How do you want to be able to respond when someone pressures you to think or feel as they do?

_____

_____

_____

_____

_____

Emotional boundaries can also be tested when someone attempts to guilt-trip you into compliance, or tries to make you responsible for *their* emotional response. How do you want to be able to respond to someone pressing your boundaries in this way?

_____

_____

_____

_____

_____

_____

_____

Sexual Boundaries

Sexual boundaries have to do with what you are comfortable with in terms of sexual expression, activity, and involvement. Sexual boundaries also encompass romantic involvement, interest or lack of interest in sexual contact, and consent. Your sexual boundaries may be challenged by people who pressure you into doing things you don't want to do, are inconsiderate or demanding as sexual partners, or who do not respect your bodily autonomy.

Assessing Your Values:
How do you express your sexuality? What feels right for you?

_____

_____

_____

_____

_____

_____

_____

What expressions of sexuality feel uncomfortable or wrong for you? Such expressions may include sexual acts, particular types of relationships (e.g., dom/sub arrangements, open relationships, monogamous relationships), or a particular gender presentation (e.g., feminine/masculine, gender assigned at birth, binary gender choices).

_____

_____

_____

_____

_____

How do you want to be able to assert sexual boundaries? How do you want to say "yes" to what is right for you and "no" to what you don't want?

_____

_____

_____

_____

_____

Social and Social Media Boundaries

Social boundaries include what you are and are not comfortable with among friends, as well as in your social media engagement. These boundaries might include which activities you feel comfortable attending, how you choose to use (or not use) social media, and how you spend your time outside work or school.

Assessing Your Values:
How important are friendships and social activities for you? Are you more introverted (recharge from alone time) or extraverted (gain energy from being around others)?

_____

_____

_____

_____

_____

Are there certain social activities you feel more comfortable doing? Are there ones that make you uncomfortable?

_____

_____

_____

_____

_____

_____

Do you use social media? If so, how do you regulate your usage (time, platforms, content, etc.)?

_____

_____

_____

_____

_____

_____

Time Boundaries

Time boundaries involve the amount of time you are willing to give to another person, project, job, or task. Your decision may include whether to take on a project, choosing how long to be involved, and when you're done with something.

Assessing Your Values:
How do you feel about giving time to people who ask for or expect it?

_____

_____

_____

_____

_____

_____

Do you feel comfortable imposing limitations, structure, or restrictions on how you give or use your time? Why or why not?

_____

_____

_____

_____

_____

Do you feel like other people have a right to your time? If so, who?

_____

_____

_____

_____

_____

Four Questions to "Yes" or "No"

Before you can decide whether a request fits within your boundaries, you have to know whether the request fits your values. Building on the "Values Assessment Exercise" in this chapter (see page 90), take a situation, whether real or imaginary, and work through whether the situation fits within your boundaries. Choose circumstances you feel likely to encounter, or may already have encountered, and answer each of the following questions to clarify your "yes" or "no."

What are my values in this situation?

Review the ways this situation tests, questions, or fits with your personal values. Which values does this situation uphold, and which does it challenge?

_____

_____

_____

_____

Does the action required in this situation fit my values?

Action may include speaking, behaving, or declining to behave in a particular manner. How do these actions or lack of actions fit with your personal values?

_____

_____

_____

_____

_____

How do I feel to be asked to do this?

Do you feel you can openly, easily, and graciously accommodate this request? Does doing so make you feel guilty? Resentful?

_____

_____

_____

_____

_____

_____

_____

Does saying "yes" or "no" feel right?

Do you have an instinctive response that feels truthful? Do you feel pressured to say "yes" when you'd rather say "no"? Do you need more time to think about it?

_____

_____

_____

_____

_____

_____

Boundary Drawing Exercise

This exercise helps you create a visual representation of your current boundaries, as well as a vision of your future. Your current boundaries may fall into one of three types: weak, rigid, or healthy. Take a look at the illustration below for a visual representation of each type of boundary:

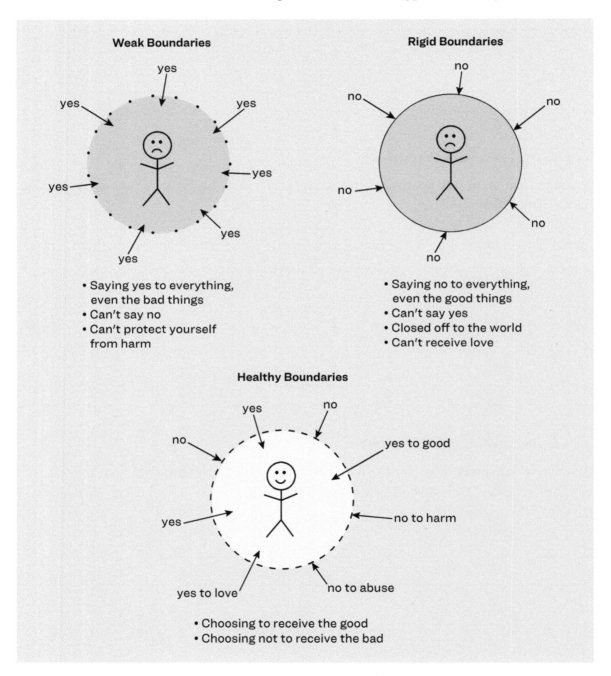

Weak Boundaries

- Saying yes to everything, even the bad things
- Can't say no
- Can't protect yourself from harm

Rigid Boundaries

- Saying no to everything, even the good things
- Can't say yes
- Closed off to the world
- Can't receive love

Healthy Boundaries

- Choosing to receive the good
- Choosing not to receive the bad

Because people and relationships are complex, your boundaries may be a combination of types. You may have weak boundaries with your children, but rigid boundaries with your spouse. Or you may have weak boundaries with a colleague, but rigid boundaries with your family.

Draw a picture of the type of boundaries (or combination of types) that you feel most represents your current boundaries. You may use different colors to depict relationships with different types of boundaries (for example, red to depict rigid boundaries, yellow for weak boundaries, green for healthy), or use different symbols to represent each type. As you draw, take note of how the different relationships and types affect you. What do you notice about your drawing?

Next, draw a picture of how you'd like your boundaries to be. How does this picture differ from the first one? What will you need to change to bring your second picture to life?

Guilt Messages Unmasked

Manipulators may show their disapproval of your boundaries by sending guilt messages. These messages are tailored to make you believe you have wronged the other person so that you will return to your previous passivity. Guilt messages are also used to cover up the individual's true feelings about your boundaries—whether that means anger, sadness, resentment, hurt, or fear. Once you recognize the true face behind the guilt mask, you can ask yourself a very important question: Is this belief stemming from my stuff, or theirs?

Boundary Guilt Bingo

Many survivors of abusive relationships have a hard time setting boundaries due to intense feelings of guilt. They believe the myths and feel that by setting boundaries they are being selfish, cruel, or rejecting. Below is a list of guilty thoughts and feelings that may interfere with your ability to set boundaries. Circle or star any that resonate for you, and write about how these thoughts and feelings affect your ability to establish boundaries in your relationships.

Saying "no" is mean.	Taking care of myself means I'm not a team player.	If I'm not agreeable, no one will like me.	If you love someone, you should be willing to do anything for them.	It's selfish to think of myself first.
I feel bad when I know someone needs something.	I don't want to hurt someone's feelings.	Other people's needs are more important than mine.	If I don't help, I am being cold and heartless.	If I set boundaries, my boss will retaliate.
My partner says I'm his everything, so I should feel the same way about him.	It feels wrong to want things. I should be grateful for what I have.	I don't want to make someone's life harder by saying "no."	I say "yes" because that's what friends are supposed to do, even if I don't really want to.	I don't want to be a burden by having my own needs.
When I try to set boundaries, people get upset. I must be doing it wrong.	You don't say "no" to family, no matter what.	Taking time for myself is taking time away from my kids.	I don't really want to lend my sister money, but I feel like I can't say "no."	Meeting my own needs first is narcissistic.
Tending to my needs first isn't fair to others.	I owe this person so much, I can't say "no" to them.	Boundaries are harsh. I feel like I should be more flexible.	I feel like I'm putting up a wall.	If I don't compromise, I'm just like my abuser.

Which of the preceding statements resonated most for you? Which did not resonate?

_____

_____

_____

_____

_____

_____

_____

_____

_____

_____

How has guilt made establishing boundaries in your life difficult?

_____

_____

_____

_____

_____

_____

_____

_____

_____

_____

_____

Family Stories

How did your family of origin feel about boundaries? As you grew through childhood, adolescence, and adulthood, did your family support you developing your unique, individual perspective? Or were you expected to abide by family or parental expectations regardless of your own beliefs? Were the rules different for different family members?

Write about how your family reacted to your attempts—or the attempts of others—to establish boundaries and individual personhood.

Example 1: *Uncle Frank was the epitome of "failure to launch." He lived with Granny until she died. He tried to move in with a girlfriend once, but the rest of the family made him feel like he was abandoning Granny, so he stayed.*

Example 2: *I wanted to go to college across the country, but my mom cried and said I was breaking her heart, so I went to community college and lived at home. I felt like such a bad daughter if I even stayed out late, because she'd wait up and tell me how worried she had been the whole time.*

_____

_____

_____

_____

_____

_____

_____

_____

_____

Timeline of You

In chapter 4, you created a timeline of your personal growth (see "History of Growth Timeline," page 64). Here, you create a timeline of your journey to finding your individuality. Beginning with your childhood, create a visual, showing each step of establishing, testing, and adjusting boundaries through the stages of development.

Your childhood years, for example, will probably include a lot of testing of what would happen if you didn't follow directions at home or school. Teen years may include more of that, plus trying out new hairstyles, hobbies and interests, and friend groups. Young adulthood may include decisions about higher education, career trajectory, and dating partners.

As you note each developmental boundary shift, also note how your family responded. Did your parents encourage four-year-old you to say "No, thank you" when you didn't want to hug a distant relative, or did they say refusing a hug was rude? Did your father threaten to throw you out of the house for getting a tattoo at 18, or did he support you in finding your own form of self-expression?

Timeline of You

TIMELINE TITLE:

Boundary Wheel

When you are unclear about what your responsibilities are (and are not), establishing effective boundaries is hard. Ultimately, boundaries always come down to managing what is within your control. But how do you know what is in your control, and what is someone else's to manage? Gaslighting blurs the lines. The gaslighter stands to benefit from coercing you into taking responsibility for things that aren't yours. The following illustration will help you clarify the differences between what you are responsible for, and what you are not:

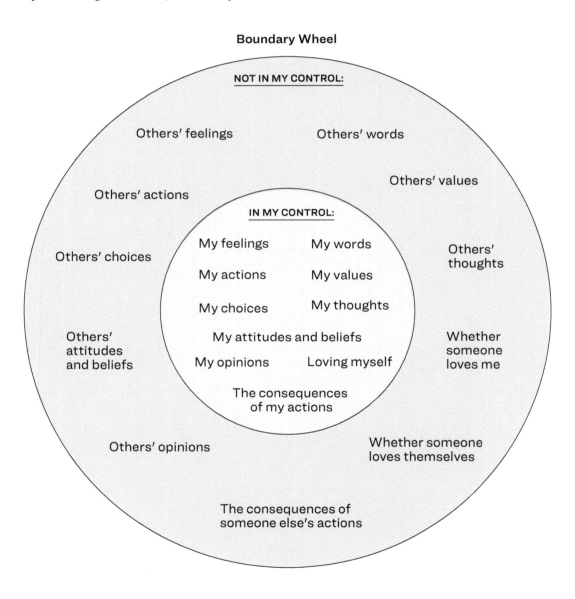

Boundary Wheel

NOT IN MY CONTROL:

Others' feelings

Others' words

Others' values

Others' actions

IN MY CONTROL:

My feelings   My words

My actions   My values

My choices   My thoughts

My attitudes and beliefs

My opinions   Loving myself

The consequences
of my actions

Others' choices

Others'
thoughts

Others'
attitudes
and beliefs

Whether
someone
loves me

Others' opinions

Whether someone
loves themselves

The consequences of
someone else's actions

What stands out to you about this visual? Where have your boundary lines become blurred? What might you need to be able to give responsibility back to someone else?

_____

_____

_____

_____

_____

Mine or Not Mine

The core of establishing boundaries in any relationship is making a clear distinction between yourself and another person. In essence, boundaries ask the question, "Is this mine, or not mine?" In this exercise, you will examine a series of vignettes and assess whether the presenting problem or concern belongs to you or the other person.

Custody Conundrum

Your ex has had her weekend with the kids, and she is two hours late bringing them home. You text her asking when she'll be back, since the kids have school the next day and she was due to return them by dinnertime. Your ex fires back, accusing you of trying to cut into her time with the kids and trying to control her.

You feel angry, but you try to calmly remind her that the custody agreement states what time the children need to be home, and that you are simply following the agreement. Your ex blames you for her feeling disconnected from the children, stating you put following the rules above building relationships. You feel bad because you know the kids miss her, and you're unsure if you are doing something wrong by asking her to follow the custody agreement.

Who is responsible for the status of your ex's relationship with your shared children?

_____

_____

_____

What about this situation is not your responsibility?

_____

_____

_____

What, if anything, are you responsible for in this situation?

_____

_____

_____

Picking Up the Slack

Your boss asks you to stay late again tonight because one of your team members fell behind in their work and a project is overdue. You don't receive overtime when you stay late, and your work was completed in a timely fashion. You know the project is important, but you resent that your boss expects you to pick up the slack for someone else. "If Jerry just did what he was supposed to, I wouldn't be eating Hot Pockets for dinner for the third night this week," you grumble as you settle back in behind your desk. Your wife will be mad, but what can you do?

Who is responsible for the lateness of the work project?

_____

_____

_____

What about this situation is someone else's concern?

_____

_____

_____

What, if anything, are you responsible for in this situation?

_____

_____

_____

Your Brother's Keeper

Your father is angry with your younger brother for defying him and getting a tattoo. Your brother is 20 years old, but your father still expects deference and total obedience. When you don't immediately join your father in condemning your brother's decision, he becomes angry at you and accuses you of encouraging your brother to disobey. He says that getting a tattoo is just the first step, and when your brother ends up homeless and on drugs, the fault will lie with you for not keeping him in line. Later, your brother calls and asks why you didn't tell your father to back off. You're now the bad guy to both people.

Who is responsible for your brother's decision to get a tattoo? For your father's emotional reaction?

_____

_____

_____

How are your boundaries being challenged in this situation?

_____

_____

_____

What, if anything, are you responsible for in this situation?

_____

_____

_____

Many people attempt to establish boundaries in the hopes of making someone else stop doing something hurtful or upsetting (see "Fact from Fiction: Separating Myths and Truths about Boundaries," page 88). The problem is, we can't control what someone else does. Setting boundaries with the goal of changing someone else is setting yourself up for disappointment.

Boundaries are not really about the other person—they are about you, and the space you need in a given relationship. Boundaries let others know what you are and are not okay with. They define where you end and the other person begins. They also communicate what you will do if the other person ignores your request to stop an upsetting or disrespectful behavior.

For this reason, they should primarily be framed as "I-statements" communicating what you will do in a particular situation (Review the "I-Statements" section in chapter 4, pages 72 to 75). For example, "I find it hurtful when you make comments about my weight. If you keep doing so, I will end the conversation." This direct statement communicates how the other person has crossed a boundary (making unwelcome and hurtful comments), how these words affect you (hurt feelings), and how you will respond if the other person does not respect your request to stop (ending the conversation).

Ground Rules for Establishing Boundaries

In addition to being focused on your own participation in a relationship, boundaries should follow a few general guidelines to be effective. Here are four basic ground rules for establishing boundaries:

1. **Articulate clear definitions.**
   Clearly state the problem. Making vague, overgeneralized statements like "You are mean" is not helpful. Identify the problematic behavior by name. "Making cruel jokes at my expense is mean" defines the problematic behavior more clearly.

2. **Be specific.**
   "You always do this/You never do that" is too broad and does not effectively convey the scope of the problem. Addressing specific behaviors, situations, or expectations strengthens your position. "You punched the door right in front of me and then denied touching it."

3. **Use I-statements.**
   Remember, boundaries are about *you* and defining your space. Use I-statements to convey how the problematic behavior infringes on your space, whether physically, mentally, emotionally, or in other ways. "When you continued to tickle me after I asked you to stop, I felt angry and disrespected. If you tickle me again, I'll get up and leave."

4. **Set sustainable consequences.**
   Establishing boundaries includes setting consequences if what you've set up is ignored. What will you do if someone does not respect the boundary you set? Be prepared with a

consequence you can consistently sustain. Instead of saying, "If you talk to me that way, I'll never speak to you again," try, "If you misgender me again after I've asked you not to, I will leave."

Levels of Contact

As much as we might wish otherwise, some will be unwilling to respect or respond to your boundaries, no matter how assertive you are, or how reasonable your boundaries may be. In these relationships, you may consider limiting the potential for harm by pulling back to a lower level of contact with that person.

Going low-contact reduces the potential for ongoing abuse by limiting how much time you spend with an abuser. In a low-contact relationship, you may skip most social functions but stay lightly connected through occasional phone calls, emails, or text messages. Low contact may be a good option for relatives, ex-spouses with whom you must co-parent, and colleagues whom you can't fully avoid.

No contact takes low-contact to its end point: cutting off or ending a relationship. You do not reach out to the other person, and you do not respond to their outreach. You may entirely avoid settings where you might see them. In extreme cases, you may move to a different city or state to get away from the person. No contact is generally reserved for cases of severe, ongoing, and unrepentant abuse.

10 Ways to Say "No" (That Aren't Mean)

Many people struggle with saying "no" because they feel like they are being mean, selfish, or uncaring. The truth is, there is nothing mean about setting a boundary. Protecting your time, energy, and space allows you to engage more willingly and graciously at a time of your choosing. An assertive "no" is better for all than a grudging "yes."

Here are 10 ways to say "no" that are not mean:

1. No.
2. That doesn't work for me.
3. Sorry, I can't do that.
4. I can't do *this* thing, but I can do *that other* thing.
5. That doesn't feel right to me.
6. I'm not okay with that.
7. Maybe another time.
8. Thanks for asking, but I have to say "no."
9. No, thank you.
10. I'd rather not.

Can you think of other ways to say "no"? Write some alternatives here.

_____

_____

_____

_____

Dealing with Pushback: Flying Monkeys

Flying monkeys are named after the creatures that attend to the Wicked Witch of the West in *The Wizard of Oz*. In the movie, the witch sends her creatures to harass and capture Dorothy, assigning them to do her dirty work for her. In relationships, flying monkeys serve as go-betweens, trying to bring newly independent friends or family members back into the fold.

Flying monkeys often reach out on behalf or at the behest of the gaslighter. They draw on the victim's sympathies and inner longing for a healthier relationship. Flying monkeys may pressure, shame, manipulate, or wheedle with victims to bring them back under the influence of the abuser. While flying monkeys may perceive themselves as peacemakers or mediators, they are usually working on behalf of the controller—the gaslighter who does not want to let their victim go.

Example: Amari felt heartsick having to set boundaries with her mother, but she couldn't take the passive-aggressive comments, veiled criticisms, and berating anymore. This would be the first Christmas she did not spend with her mom. Though she knew her decision not to go was right, she was deeply saddened.

A few days before Christmas, Amari got a phone call from her aunt, asking if she was coming home for Christmas. When Amari explained she needed some space from her mom, her aunt scolded her for punishing her mother by leaving her alone at Christmas. Amari hung up the phone and cried. The next day, she got another call—this time from her grandmother. "Amari," her Mom-mom said, "Your mother isn't perfect, but you are taking this too far. Come home and work it out with her." The calls and texts from relatives continued until the day before Christmas, but Amari's mother never called.

Amari experienced flying monkeys in the form of her aunt, grandmother, and other relatives.

Have you encountered flying monkeys in your relationships? Write about your experience(s) here.

_____

_____

_____

_____

Dealing with Pushback, Part 2: Get-in-Line Messages

Get-in-line messages are subtle or overt messages to get you to return to your usual place within the gaslighter's sphere of influence. Flying monkeys may employ get-in-line messages if appealing to your sympathies doesn't work. These messages are an attempt to shame you into submission.

Example: Jacob had been close with his father as a boy, but their relationship became strained due to his father's substance abuse. He covered for his father's drunk driving and other dangerous choices many times, but eventually decided he couldn't continue. The next time his father got into an accident due to driving under the influence, Jacob did not come to help. His father called Jacob's younger brother, Seth, who drove out to pull their father's car out of a ditch.

Jacob was caught off guard when Seth appeared on his doorstep after midnight that night, fuming. "How could you leave me to deal with Dad and just sit here on your couch watching TV?" he demanded. "I just spent hours getting his car out of the ditch and making sure he didn't have a concussion, and you can't be bothered to help? How selfish are you? I can't believe you wouldn't help your own family." Jacob reminded Seth he had performed these very tasks for years without complaint, but Seth didn't care. "You don't get to walk out on family," he said angrily. "If this situation happens again, you better come out and help or the whole family will know what kind of a person you really are."

Seth shamed Jacob and accused him of selfishness in an attempt to pressure him back into his old role as family enabler and problem-solver.

Have you encountered get-in-line messages in your relationships? Write about your experience(s) here.

_____

_____

_____

_____

_____

_____

Recognizing the Subtle Signs

When you have grown up in or spent a lot of time in relationships with poor boundaries, discerning when your boundaries have been disrespected can be difficult. Doing so isn't always as obvious as drawing a line in the sand and telling someone not to take a step, then watching them tap dance across the line with a "so what?"

Paying attention to the subtle signs can help clue you in to when your boundaries are being unconsciously challenged. Think about a time something felt uncomfortable, somehow wrong, or just plain *off*. You may have had a vague sense something wasn't right, but not much clarity on what exactly was wrong. Examine that memory with the following questions:

What emotions did I have in that situation?

_____

_____

_____

_____

_____

What thoughts did I have in that situation?

_____

_____

_____

_____

_____

What physical sensations did I have in that situation?

_____

_____

_____

_____

_____

Which of my value(s) were being ignored, downplayed, or disrespected in that situation?

_____

_____

_____

_____

_____

Boundary Stomping

On the other end of the spectrum, boundary stomps are anything but subtle. A boundary stomp occurs when someone interprets your establishment of a boundary as a personal affront. Boundary stompers believe their wishes and desires supersede all others. They will see the lines you set up as a challenge and may toe that line many times before finally stomping over the line and provoking a response. The gaslighter may then use your response to gaslight you, particularly if they characterize the response as over-the-top.

Some examples of boundary stomping include:

* The mother-in-law who ignores your instructions about how to feed your baby, giving her ice cream after you tell her the baby is not ready to start solid foods.
* The boyfriend who insists on ordering for you at restaurants, though he always orders seafood knowing you hate it. He is sure you will come to love the seafood as much as he does if you (are forced to) eat it enough.
* The friend who borrows your car and changes all your preset radio stations or signs you up for a satellite radio program subscription on your dollar.
* The boss who repeatedly expects you to handle work problems on your days off, emailing or calling you constantly until you stop what you were doing to attend to the problem.

How have you encountered boundary stomping in your life?

_____

_____

_____

_____

_____

How did you respond to it?

_____

_____

_____

_____

_____

Engage, Disengage, or Make a Strategic Retreat

The last few exercises have explored different ways people in your life may fail to respect the boundaries you set. This exercise presents three options for responding when your boundaries are disrespected or ignored. When someone challenges your boundaries, you have three basic choices: engage, disengage, or make a strategic retreat.

Engage: Sometimes you may choose to address the other person in the moment. You may point out how they are crossing a boundary, explain why respecting what you've laid out is important, or remind them of the consequences if they do not stop what they're doing. If they argue or ask why it matters, you might explain or simply reiterate your stance (review the "Rinse and Repeat" responses you created in chapter 4, pages 81 and 82).

Imagine a situation where your boundaries are crossed and you'd like to engage.

_____

_____

_____

_____

_____

Disengage: There will be times when someone challenges a boundary and you know nothing will be gained by discussing the situation. You can disengage from dead-end conversations by hanging up the phone, walking away, not replying to a text message, or changing the subject. When a gaslighter tries to bait you by challenging your perception of events, you might disengage by stating, "We remember what happened differently. There doesn't seem to be a need to continue discussing this issue."

Think of a situation where you would prefer to disengage.

_____

_____

_____

_____

_____

Strategic Retreat: When you know you will be entering a situation where gaslighting, flying monkeys, boundary stomping, or get-in-line messages are likely to occur, consider leaving yourself room for a strategic retreat. Park your car at the end of the lot or stand near a doorway so you have the option of leaving. If a disagreement is escalating and you feel unsafe, you are not obligated to stay and continue to be abused.

Think of a situation where you might need a strategic retreat.

_____

_____

_____

_____

_____

_____

Building On Your History

There is a first time for everything, including setting boundaries. Think about your previous attempts to establish boundaries in relationships. Even if you don't think you did a good job, or if they seemed unsuccessful, those early attempts are the seeds of learning how to hold space for yourself.

What kinds of boundaries have you tried to set in the past?

_____

_____

_____

_____

_____

What went well in your previous attempts?

_____

_____

_____

_____

_____

What did not go well?

_____

_____

_____

_____

_____

What would you do differently now?

_____

_____

_____

_____

_____

What did you learn about yourself and the other person in this situation?

_____

_____

_____

_____

_____

What boundaries do you want to set in your life now?

_____

_____

_____

_____

_____

What can you do differently now, knowing what you do?

_____

_____

_____

_____

_____

Permission to Leave/Permission to Stay

When abuse is ongoing, and chances of anything changing are slim-to-none, you can make your strategic retreat a permanent one. Although society has many messages about family, commitment, and community, your safety and well-being come first. The decision can be difficult and deeply painful, but some relationships cannot be salvaged.

What would need to happen for you to end a relationship? Where is your line in the sand? What do you need to say to yourself to feel like you can walk away from an abusive or destructive relationship?

My line in the sand is:

_____

_____

_____

_____

_____

_____

I give myself permission to walk away because:

_____

_____

_____

_____

_____

_____

You may have relationships from which you feel unable or unwilling to walk away. If you choose to stay, think about what you need that relationship to look like in order for you to be safe. How can you make your situation the best possible scenario?

My reasons to stay:

_____

_____

_____

I give myself permission to:

_____

_____

_____

Protective Visualization

There may be times when you cannot avoid spending time with someone who challenges your emotional and mental boundaries. For those times, this visualization can help you remember you do not need to accept their incursion into your space. You may perform this brief meditation before you see the boundary-pusher, or as soon as you sense them challenging your boundaries in the moment.

Begin by becoming aware of the physical boundary of your skin. Notice how there's a clear line between where your body starts and stops in space. Now imagine a clear, flexible, but strong coating covering your skin. The covering is porous, allowing air and positive energy to flow through to you, but resisting negative energy.

Next imagine a clear cylinder or dome descending over the boundary-pusher. The dome is sealed, preventing them from leaving their defined space and entering yours. Their negative energy, gaslighting, guilt-tripping, and other manipulations are all held inside the dome with them. Although they may attempt to break through the dome and invade your boundaries, your invisible coating protects you. Ultimately, they are left inside the dome with whatever energy they have brought with them.

Affirming Your Space

Create at least five affirmations or mantras that support your right to occupy and hold space, establish boundaries, and be your own person. Speak what you seek into existence. Offer gratitude to the universe, or whatever resonates for you spiritually, for supporting your boundaries.

Examples:

"I deserve to establish boundaries that serve me in my life."

"Every day I become clearer and clearer about the boundaries I want and need."

"I can easily communicate my boundaries and have them respected."

Your Turn:

_____

_____

_____

_____

_____

Review and Wrap-Up

Look back at the exercises in this chapter.

What resonated with you the most?

_____

_____

What did not resonate?

_____

_____

How do you feel right now? Have your feelings changed since you started this chapter?

_____

_____

What will you take away from these exercises?

_____

_____

PART III

HEALING FROM TRAUMA

The ultimate goal of recovering from gaslighting is to heal the wounds you received in an abusive relationship. As you have worked through the first two parts, you have developed an understanding of how you have been hurt by gaslighting, how your pain has affected you in relationships, and how to protect yourself from further abuse. Now you turn your attention to the places in you that are ready to heal. Part III of this workbook focuses on healing by practicing self-care and learning what a healthy relationship looks and feels like.

CHAPTER 6

Self-Care

As you move into the final phase of this workbook, take a moment to congratulate yourself for the hard work you've done thus far. You have learned to identify gaslighting by definition, as well as by its signs, symptoms, and lingering effects. You have explored the impact gaslighting has had on you personally and begun to heal by developing self-compassion, assertiveness, and rebuilding your self-esteem. The journey from victim to survivor can be a bumpy one. You deserve to feel proud of yourself for each step of that journey.

In this chapter, you develop a self-care routine to support your growth and healing. A number of exercises here are designed to help you clarify your self-care needs, identify barriers to self-care, and promote a healthier lifestyle.

Remember, meeting your own needs is not selfish. Taking care of yourself in this way is, in fact, critical to being a whole and healthy person. Knowing that you *can* do something and knowing *how* to do it, however, are two different things. That is the purpose of this chapter: To give you new insights, new ideas, and new options for taking care of you.

Let's begin!

REALMS OF SELF-CARE

Self-care includes five main realms: physical, mental, emotional, spiritual, and relational.

Physical self-care refers to caring for your physical body. This type of care includes getting adequate rest, eating nutritious food, drinking enough water, getting enough exercise, treating illness or injuries, and engaging in positive touch.

Mental self-care refers to caring for your mind. This type of care includes learning new things, challenging and changing problematic thought patterns, developing informed opinions, resting from mental labor such as work, and using your brain in ways you enjoy.

Emotional self-care refers to caring for your heart. This type of care includes connecting to and validating your feelings, healing emotional wounds, expressing your feelings constructively, and doing things that make your heart full.

Spiritual self-care refers to caring for your spirit. This type of care may, but does not have to, include religious beliefs and practices. Spiritual self-care includes meditation, mindfulness, setting intentions, affirmations, and practicing gratitude.

Relational self-care refers to caring for yourself within relationships. This type of care includes making decisions about whom you spend time with, retaining individuality within a partnership, nurturing loving relationships, and ending or changing harmful relationships.

You may notice the overlap in several of these realms. People are complex and multifaceted; because these realms touch on one another, caring for yourself in one realm can have a ripple effect of positive energy into another. For example, rubbing a scented lotion onto your skin may make your skin feel soft, while also evoking pleasant memories associated with the scent, making you feel happy and contented. Reading a great book may open your mind to new concepts, take you through a range of emotional experiences, and give you something to talk about at your next social gathering.

This exercise helps you establish a primary realm of self-care for a number of activities you identify—but don't worry if your exercises touch on multiple realms as this just means you're getting more for your self-care buck!

Write down your five favorite forms of self-care at this time. What realm(s) do your favorites fall into? Are there any realms you're currently neglecting?

_____

_____

_____

_____

_____

Self-Care Is More

To be really effective, self-care needs to be more than flopping down on the couch and bingeing on Netflix all weekend. The occasional lazy day can be fun, but it's not enough by itself to help you refresh and reset. As you begin establishing your self-care routine, keep the following core principles in mind. Self-care is:

Connected: At its core, self-care is about connecting to your own needs, wants, and well-being. If your self-care does not make you feel more in tune with yourself, some adjustment may be needed.

Active: Self-care is ideally a proactive process—a part of your daily life, rather than something you fall back on when you're already tired. Look for small ways to actively care for yourself each day, rather than waiting until you feel overwhelmed and exhausted.

Rejuvenating: Self-care should be something that restores the energy you spend on everything else. Even if your method of self-care leaves you physically tired, you should feel refreshed in spirit.

Expansive: Self-care will grow and deepen with you. As an active, evolving process, your self-care will change as you grow and develop. If your usual methods of self-care are leaving you bored, stagnant, or unchanged, it's time to try something new.

Physical Self-Care: Rest, Recover, and Refresh

If you ask a random sampling of people how they practice self-care, a sizable majority would likely name *resting* as one of their favorites. Work, school, exercise, hobbies, family obligations, social engagements, social media posts, housework, commuting time, keeping up with the news . . . in any given day, you might be inundated with busyness and activity from the moment your eyes open in the morning until they close in sleep at night. As a society, we are increasingly busy, increasingly anxious, and increasingly exhausted.

Small wonder, then, that so many of us crave rest! And rest is an important factor in practicing physical self-care. Getting enough rest allows us to physically recover from our day, restore the energy depleted by our comings and goings, and feel refreshed. Use the following questions to gauge whether you are getting enough rest:

How many hours of sleep do you need each night to feel truly rested and ready to wake up in the morning?

How many hours of sleep do you actually get?

_____

If you are not getting enough, what interferes with your sleep?

_____

Name at least one behavioral change you can implement immediately to improve your rest (e.g., no screens for an hour before bed, use a blue light filter if you do have screens, no caffeine past 1 p.m., etc.).

_____

_____

Rest does not only mean sleeping. Taking time off to heal from an illness or injury, sitting quietly in a meditative pose, and pausing to breathe slowly and deeply can all be ways of resting your body. Name at least three other ways you can rest.

_____

_____

_____

Physical Self-Care: Get Moving

On the other side of the coin, your body was made to move. Whatever your level of athleticism, physical ability/mobility, or restrictions, finding ways to move your body can be a means of self-care. Even for those with physical disabilities and chronic pain conditions such as fibromyalgia, incorporating some movement into each day can improve symptoms significantly.

Use the following questions to energize your physical self-care:

What kinds of physical activities do you enjoy? Activity does not have to mean formal exercise. Anything that gets you in motion and feels good will do.

_____

_____

_____

How often do you engage in these activities?

_____

_____

If you do not engage in them very often, what stops you?

_____

_____

Name at least one behavioral change you can implement immediately to increase your physical activity by 10%:

_____

_____

Sometimes, people are afraid to engage in physical activities they find challenging. But pursuing a challenge can be exciting and invigorating, even if hard! Identify at least one physical activity you find challenging or a little scary, and make a plan to try that activity at least once in the next month.

Example: *I will attend the next beginner's rock climbing class at my local climbing gym, this Friday at 6 p.m. I will pack my gym clothes and leave them in the car so I can go right after work.*

_____

_____

Mental Self-Care: Take a Break

You've probably heard (and used) the phrase "zoning out" to describe the practice of taking a mental break. Zoning out is a valid option for creating mental distance from a problem, but there are additional ways to achieve this distance. Use the following questions to explore other ways to take a mental break:

What kinds of tasks or situations do you find mentally draining?

_____

_____

When do you feel like you need a mental break? When do you become most mentally tired?

_____

_____

When do your thoughts run away with you?

Example: *I can't stop running through my to-do list at night to see what I missed.*

_____

_____

Name at least one way to give yourself a mental break without completely zoning out.

Example: *When my mind starts racing, I will write my thoughts on a notepad I keep by the bed so that I don't have to keep track of everything in my head.*

_____

_____

Mental Self-Care: Go Deeper

Sometimes, mental self-care means doing the opposite of zoning out: tuning in and going deeper. Reading self-help books (like this one!), learning a new skill or developing an existing one, journaling, and engaging in respectful debate are all ways of deepening your thinking. And engaging your mind in stimulating, interesting tasks is a form of mental self-care.

Use the following questions to explore how you can engage, deepen, and expand your mind:

What kinds of activities, prompts, exercises, or questions interest you? What do you find mentally stimulating?

_____

_____

_____

What areas do you feel knowledgeable about? What would you like to learn more about?

_____

_____

_____

What is at least one question (silly or serious) you've always wanted to have answered? Look up the answer and briefly write out your response here:

Question:

_____

_____

Answer:

_____

_____

Name at least one skill you would like to learn, deepen, or expand. Identify a resource to begin learning about this skill.

Example: *I want to learn to play the guitar. I will find a YouTube video and learn one chord this week.*

_____

_____

_____

Self-Care Is Not Selfish

Survivors of emotional abuse sometimes worry that taking time to attend to their own needs means they are being selfish. Has this worry ever kept you from taking care of yourself? If so, take heart. Practicing self-care does not mean you are ignoring or trampling the needs of others for your own benefit. Taking care of yourself is vital to being present and lovingly engaged in your relationships.

Emotional Self-Care: Acknowledge, Validate, and Befriend

One of the first casualties in a gaslighting relationship is your freedom of emotional expression. Gaslighters question, criticize, and invalidate your feelings to keep you off-balance. Your ability to care for your emotional health takes a hit when you are constantly told your feelings are wrong. Emotional self-care involves unlearning that message and replacing what you've been repeatedly told with internal validation.

When you have an emotional response, pause and notice what you are actually feeling. Name the emotion(s) here.

Example: *I am really upset after fighting with my girlfriend. I am angry, sad, and embarrassed.*

_____

_____

_____

When you notice yourself having no feelings, be curious about what is happening. What are you not allowing yourself to feel?

Example: *I go blank when my girlfriend berates me. It's better not to feel anything than to be hurt and angry.*

_____

_____

_____

Validate your emotional experience, regardless of what that experience is.

Example: *I am feeling really angry right now, and my anger is valid.*

_____

_____

_____

Befriend your feelings. They are telling you about how you experience a relationship.

Example: *I appreciate my anger because it tells me when someone is crossing my boundaries. Thank you, anger.*

_____

_____

_____

EMOTIONAL SELF-CARE: HEAL AND RELEASE

Acknowledging, validating, and befriending your emotions is an important piece of emotional self-care. Additionally, naming and owning your feelings is a powerful act of self-love that counteracts the self-erasing messages of gaslighting. But sometimes we can become stuck in difficult feelings and prolong the pain, putting off healing. Feelings of helplessness, bitterness, resentment, and hopelessness can make moving forward in your life hard. Here is where releasing comes in.

Note: Healing and releasing is a process. You may need to repeat this exercise several times to feel a release. Healing and releasing pain are also ideal goals with which to begin psychotherapy. Don't be afraid to start your work here and continue with a healing professional.

Healing and Releasing Meditation

Settle into a comfortable position, either seated or lying down. Close your eyes and bring your attention inward. Notice your breathing, and take a moment to simply follow your breath moving in and out of your body. Notice if your breath feels smooth, open, and free, or constrained, rapid, and shallow. Remain with your breath until it feels smooth and easy.

Bring your awareness to your heart. Invite the light at the center of your being to fill your heart. Feel both the light and your breath as they fill, move through, and illuminate your heartspace. Feel your heart expand with all the love, light, and self-compassion it can hold.

Invite the parts of you that carry pain to step into the light around your heart. As each wounded part enters the light, welcome it. With each breath and with each beat of your heart, send your wounded parts love and light. Invite those wounded parts to rest in your heartspace for as long as they wish. Allow them to share with you any stories, beliefs, or memories of the wounds they may carry.

When it feels right, invite your wounded parts to release any shame, blame, grief, or anger they feel about their wounding, if they are willing. If they are not willing, that is okay. They don't need to do anything until and unless they feel ready.

If a wounded part does wish to release something, this part may send that pain away from itself in whatever way feels best. Burn or bury the pain, scatter it to the wind, shoot it into the heart of the sun—whatever feels best for that part of you. In the space where the wounded part held that pain is room to invite in the love and light of your heart.

As your heart heals, its capacity for love, light, and self-compassion will grow. Thank your heart for its infinite capacity for healing. Finish this meditation by sitting in gratitude.

SPIRITUAL SELF-CARE: CONNECT AND TAKE IN

Spiritual self-care entails tending to the needs of your spirit. Spiritual care may, but does not have to, include religious practices or prayers. Tending to the spirit may include meditation, contemplation, or setting intentions for yourself. Gratitude, mindfulness, and affirmations are all forms of spiritual self-care.

For this exercise, you will focus on connecting with environments that soothe your spirit. Find a physical location that invokes feelings of peace, connection, and positive energy. For many, this location will have an abundance of nature—somewhere like a park, meadow, forest, or quiet beach. You may sit, stand, lie down, or walk.

Connect and Take In

Begin by focusing on what your five senses tell you about your environment. Notice the sounds of the wind, your footsteps on the ground, the temperature and scent of the air. Take a sip of water, and focus all of your attention on the sensation of the liquid on your lips, tongue, and throat.

As you walk, feel yourself as a part of nature. Feel connected to the earth through your feet. Feel your head brush the sky. Feel your body move through the air. Lean in to your connection to the world.

Listen to the sounds of your passage—your footsteps crunching on leaves, gravel, or sand; your arms as they brush past bushes or rub against your sides; your breath as it enters and exits your body. Hear how your existence adds to the sounds of life in the world.

Find a comfortable place to sit or lie on the ground. Feel the sun on your body. Feel gravity holding you to the earth. Hear the subtle movements of insects in the soil, and the distant beat of birds' wings in the wind. Hear the buzz of the bees and chattering of squirrels. Take in the thread of energy that connects you to the community of living, breathing beings. Welcome your connection to nature.

Spiritual Self-Care: Brush It Off

Spiritual self-care also includes releasing and freeing yourself of energy that drains or hurts your spirit. In the previous exercise, you welcomed and opened up to nature, feeling your connection to the world. In this exercise, you will rid yourself of what does not serve your spirit.

Sit or stand as tall as you can, with your back straight and head high. Imagine the energy of negative beliefs, negative self-talk, and negative experiences as black tendrils touching your skin. Now imagine your heartlight growing from within, pressing through your skin and breaking the contact with those tendrils. Breathe deeply as your heartlight moves through you, loosening the tendrils and filling you with love and light.

Lay your right hand on your left shoulder, and with a firm, energized motion, sweep your hand down your arm. Brush the tendrils away, continuing the motion down your arms and off the ends of your fingertips. Set the intention to brush off the negative energy that drains your spirit. Repeat the brushing motion as many times as you need until you feel cleared of the negative energy around your left arm. If you find the brushing motion physically difficult, visualize this action instead.

Repeat the brushing motion, this time using your left hand to brush off your right arm. Brush both arms down your upper and lower legs, down your trunk, and from the top of your head to your shoulders. Continually hold the intention of releasing negative energy.

Now take in a slow, deep breath through your nose, expanding your chest and belly as they fill with air. With a short, sharp, explosive exhalation, release your breath and use your diaphragm to forcefully push the air out through your mouth.

Use your hands to emphasize the motion of pushing air away from you. Form a slight contraction in your abdomen as you exhale. Repeat the inhalation and exhalation until you feel clear and open inside. If you become dizzy, hold your breath for a few seconds between inhaling and exhaling. Finish this exercise by sitting or standing tall and firm, breathing normally, and visualize yourself filled with heartlight.

Relational Self-Care: Deepen and Nurture

Relational self-care refers to how you take care of yourself within relationships. One important aspect of relational self-care is investing in, nurturing, and deepening relationships that nourish you. Think about the people in your life who make you feel loved, supported, and validated. How can you increase your connection to these people?

Name three or more people who support, love, and validate you.

_____

_____

_____

_____

_____

_____

How do these relationships nourish you?

_____

_____

_____

_____

_____

How much time do you spend with people who nourish you? How do you engage with these nourishing relationships?

_____

_____

_____

Identify at least one opportunity to nurture these loving relationships every day.

_____

_____

_____

_____

Thank your loved ones for nurturing you with their love, support, and validation. How can you express your appreciation?

_____

_____

_____

_____

Relational Self-Care: Detach and Disengage

Some relationships do not nurture you. Relational self-care includes creating distance between yourself and those relationships that drain or harm you. All relationships bring pain to some degree, as conflict, disagreement, mistakes, and hurt are all normal to some level. But toxic or abusive relationships are disproportionately skewed toward these harmful experiences. How can you limit your exposure to relationships that wound you?

Which relationships in your life bring you the most pain? Identify at least one relationship that is toxic, abusive, or disproportionately negative.

_____

_____

_____

How does this relationship hurt you?

_____

_____

_____

_____

_____

_____

How much time do you spend with people who hurt you? How much do you have to engage with these relationships?

_____

_____

_____

_____

_____

_____

Identify opportunities you have to detach or disengage from toxic interactions, relationships, and environments. When can you walk away, decline an invitation, or leave an interaction?

_____

_____

_____

_____

_____

_____

Self-Care Is Necessary for Healing

The most damaging, lingering effect of emotional abuse is the way it disconnects you from your sense of self. Gaslighting disconnects you from what anchors you in your life: *you*. Self-care is a necessary step in your healing and recovery process that allows you to reconnect you to yourself in a loving, compassionate, and validating way. Practicing self-care reaffirms to yourself that your needs are valid, your wants are acceptable, and you are worthy of love and attention.

Introvert/Extravert

Introversion and extraversion refer to the way a person responds to social engagement with others. *Introverts* find social engagement tiring and recharge their batteries by spending time alone. They often prefer small groups or one-on-one involvement when they socialize. *Extraverts* find socialization energizing and recharge their batteries by spending time with other people. They often enjoy being in the middle of the action, with plenty of people with whom they can talk and engage.

Depending on whether you are more introverted or extraverted, your self-care needs may look a little different. Introverts tend to prioritize self-care that does not require them to be around other people as much. Extraverts may be less refreshed by self-care that does not involve other people. Take the quiz below to find out which side you fall on, and plan your self-care accordingly. For each statement, circle "Me" if the statement applies to you and "Not me" if the statement does not represent you.

1. I am often perceived as social and outgoing.
   Me   Not me
2. I am often perceived as reserved and introspective.
   Me   Not me
3. I enjoy being among and working in groups of people.
   Me   Not me
4. I prefer being around one or two people at a time. Groups make me uncomfortable.
   Me   Not me
5. I dislike being alone.
   Me   Not me
6. I value my alone time and enjoy my own company.
   Me   Not me
7. I have a large group of friends and acquaintances.
   Me   Not me
8. I know a few people very well.
   Me   Not me

9. I can jump quickly into a new activity or interest, sometimes at the expense of thinking things all the way through.

   Me   Not me

10. I sometimes overthink new opportunities and may move too slowly.

    Me   Not me

11. I sometimes forget to stop and think about what I want and what I am trying to achieve before starting a new project.

    Me   Not me

12. I sometimes forget to check whether my ideas and inner experience fit with the outside world.

    Me   Not me

If you answered "Me" on four or more odd-numbered questions, you scored higher on extraversion than introversion. Emphasize self-care activities that involve being around people. If you answered "Me" on four or more even-numbered questions, you scored higher on introversion. Your self-care will be more focused on time with yourself or a very few close friends. If your answers are evenly split between odds and evens, you may be an *ambivert*—meaning you draw equal or nearly equal satisfaction from activities suited to introverts or extraverts. Structure your self-care routine to draw equally from both sides.

Full Focus

On some level, you are already practicing a certain amount of daily self-care. You feed and clothe yourself, go to sleep at night, spend time with friends and loved ones, and enjoy your favorite hobbies and interests. When self-care becomes routine, we sometimes stop noticing its effects on our mood. This exercise will help you mindfully refocus on your daily self-care.

Choose an activity of daily self-care, such as eating a meal, taking a shower, or putting on your pajamas. Focus your full attention on what you are doing. Using as many of your senses as possible, observe every detail you can about the activity as you work through it. Note your mood before engaging in this activity, as well as during and afterward. What do you notice?

Self-care activity:

_____

_____

_____

_____

Mood before starting:

_____

_____

_____

_____

Observations using all senses:

_____

_____

_____

_____

Details you notice:

_____

_____

_____

_____

Mood after completion:

_____

_____

_____

_____

ELEVATE THE MUNDANE

Choose a daily self-care activity to make special. If you normally take a five-minute shower with no frills, give yourself an extra ten minutes to stand under the hot water and relax. If you normally scarf down lunch while sending work emails, turn off your phone or laptop and eat lunch in a quiet, pleasant space. If you usually throw whatever leftovers you have on a plate and call the meal good enough, take some time to prepare a full, delicious meal and then savor the tastes. Bring mindful attention to what you often do without thinking, and make your daily self-care a little more special.

10 Ideas for Self-Care Activities

Now it's your turn to create an environment that supports you in caring for yourself. Try to give some attention every day to each of the five realms—physical, mental, emotional, spiritual, and relational. Still not sure what self-care looks like? Here are 10 great ideas to get you started:

- **Snuggle a pet.** Pets are good for your health—mental, emotional, and physical!
- **Call or meet up with a friend.** Spend time with people who love and support you.
- **Complete one small household task you've been putting off.** Relieve stress and achieve satisfaction by knocking something off your to-do list.
- **Get outside in the sunlight.** Sunshine is good for the soul—and most of us can use a little more vitamin D.
- **Do your favorite leisure activity, such as a jigsaw puzzle, art activity, playing an instrument, or listening to music.** Having fun is an act of self-care.
- **Try a new activity or class.** You may find a new favorite hobby!
- **Dance.** You don't need training to move your body. Put on your favorite songs and rock out!
- **Read a book for fun.** A great book can take you anywhere you want to go.
- **Redecorate or rearrange a corner of your living space.** Make your space a haven.
- **Go on an adventure.** Take a hike, go kayaking, explore a new city, or drive somewhere just for the sake of going.

Review and Wrap-Up

Look back at the exercises in this chapter.

What resonated with you the most?

_____

_____

_____

_____

_____

What did not resonate?

_____

_____

_____

_____

_____

How do you feel right now? Have your feelings changed since you started this chapter?

_____

_____

_____

_____

_____

What will you take away from these exercises?

_____

_____

_____

_____

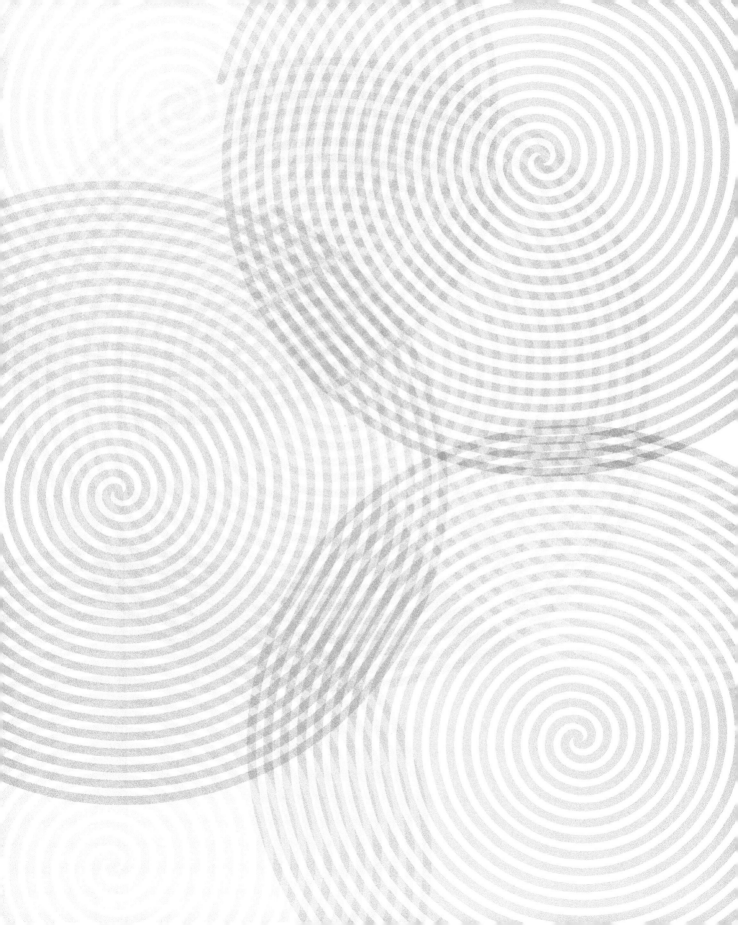

CHAPTER 7

Establishing Healthy Relationships

O ver the last six chapters, you have examined—in great detail—what your unhealthy relationships look like. Now you build upon everything you've learned to create a healthier future. Chapter 7 has exercises and writing prompts designed to help you develop a clearer picture of the healthy relationships you want to build moving forward.

Understanding what has happened to you and how it happened is an important first step in recovering from trauma and abuse. But this recovery does not stop at understanding past experiences. Recovery happens when you can take what you know about yourself and your relationships and use that understanding to create a healthier future.

Let's begin.

Completing the Picture

Sometimes the most interesting artwork directs our focus somewhere unexpected. We may start out looking at one aspect of an intriguing image, only to find our gaze drawn to a completely different area within the piece. Allowing our gaze to be drawn away from the immediate or obvious area of focus allows us to see a more complete, detailed, and nuanced image.

As we begin exploring the relationships we wish to change, we can become very focused on the unhealthy relationships that caused us to first begin examining this picture. Identifying unhealthy situations is an important skill, however, if we stop at only identifying our toxic relationships, we miss another crucial element of the bigger picture: the texture of a healthy relationship. As with art, we obtain a more complete picture by learning to see what wasn't immediately in focus upon first glance.

This exercise allows you to begin exploring what a healthy relationship looks like by identifying traits that are the opposite of the toxic and unhealthy ones with which you are familiar. Begin by drawing your attention to a toxic or unhealthy aspect, then identify the opposite—a healthier trait that would be present in a positive relationship.

For each of the 10 toxic relationship traits listed below, counter with at least one healthy relationship trait.

Example:

Toxic Trait: Brutal honesty

Opposite Healthy Trait: Honesty with kindness

TOXIC TRAIT	OPPOSITE HEALTHY TRAIT
Gaslighting	
Jealousy	
Dishonesty	
Lack of empathy	
Codependency	
Unequal distribution of power	
Manipulation/coercion	
Violence	
Pressure to comply	
Refusal to compromise	

QUALITIES OF HEALTHY RELATIONSHIPS

Just as certain traits, behaviors, attitudes, and expectations can create a toxic or abusive relationship, other traits, behaviors, attitudes, and expectations support healthy relationships. Seven core qualities provide the structure for such healthy relationships. Let's take a look:

1. **Mutual Respect**
   In a healthy relationship, both parties have a basic level of respect for each other as human beings. When you respect someone, you treat them well.

2. **Trust**
   Relationships flourish when each person is able to trust the other. Trust is earned, and if broken, the breach must be healed before the relationship can grow again.

3. **Compassion**
   Compassion is the recognition of and concern for another person's pain. Compassion does not mean you try to fix someone's problems for them, but that you care about their suffering.

4. **Assertive Communication**
   In a healthy relationship, both parties openly and clearly communicate their thoughts and feelings while respecting and caring about the other person's thoughts and feelings.

5. **Compromise**
   In a healthy relationship, both parties are willing to proactively address conflict, working together to find a mutually satisfying compromise.

6. **Honesty and Authenticity**
   Being compassionately truthful with each other allows both individuals to be open and authentic in the relationship. Authenticity promotes the core qualities of trust and respect.

7. **Healthy Boundaries**
   Contrary to Hollywood messages like "You complete me," the best and strongest relationships embrace individuality and healthy boundaries.

Healthy Relationship Quiz

How healthy are your relationships? Take the following quiz and find out! Read each question carefully, and check the box that describes your relationships most accurately. You may use this quiz to assess friendships, family relationships, or professional relationships. Directions for scoring can be found at the end of the exercise.

My person in this relationship:

		ALWAYS	OFTEN	SOMETIMES	RARELY	NEVER
1.	Is supportive of my goals and interests					
2.	Encourages me to try new things					
3.	Listens to my concerns					
4.	Respects my boundaries					
5.	Supports me having a life outside of our relationship					
6.	Cares about my feelings					
7.	Accepts my "no"					
8.	Is kind to me					
9.	Says I am too sensitive					
10.	Thinks I need to learn to take criticism better					
11.	Doesn't admit to mistakes or wrongdoing					
12.	Doesn't like when I spend time with other people					
13.	Makes me feel stupid, unattractive, unlovable, or unworthy					
14.	Wears me down or makes me feel guilty when I try to say "no"					
15.	Is mean, disrespectful, or unkind to me					
16.	Makes me question my sanity, experiences, and/ or judgment					

Scoring:

Use the key below to score your responses. Pay careful attention. Scoring is different for the first and second half of the quiz.

Questions 1–8:

Always = 4 pts
Often = 3 pts
Sometimes = 2 pts
Rarely = 1 pt
Never = 0 pts

Questions 9–16:

Always = 0 pts
Often = 1 pt
Sometimes = 2 pts
Rarely = 3 pts
Never = 4 pts

43 to 64 pts: Your relationship is pretty healthy! This relationship includes largely positive interactions, traits, and behaviors, and relatively few hurtful or harmful practices.

22 to 42 pts: Your relationship is fair. This relationship includes some thoughtful and respectful behaviors, as well as some areas of concern. If you can advocate for your needs and if the other person is willing to put some work in, there is room to improve.

0 to 21 pts: Your relationship is showing several red flags. Your person does not demonstrate caring and supportive behaviors and may behave in harmful or abusive ways. While there may be some chance of improvement, this relationship is currently unhealthy.

Relationships in Real Life

Think about the unhealthiest or most toxic relationship in your life (past or present). Write about what makes or made this relationship unhealthy, in detail. What toxic traits, behaviors, and patterns do/did you see?

_____

_____

_____

_____

_____

_____

_____

_____

_____

Now think about the healthiest relationship you have witnessed or experienced. Write in detail about what makes or made this relationship healthy. What traits, behaviors, and patterns do/did you see? What makes/made this relationship different from the unhealthy one(s)?

_____

_____

_____

_____

_____

Relationship Role Models

Think about the people in your life whose relationships you admire. These relationships could be familial, such as among siblings or between a parent and child, platonic, romantic, or professional. What do you admire about these relationships? What aspects would you like to use as a model for your own relationships?

_____

_____

_____

_____

Tuning In

For many survivors of abuse, one of the challenges of building new, healthier relationships is learning to trust their instincts again. Gaslighting can be so effective at teaching victims to question, dismiss, or shove down their responses to toxic behavior, they may feel unable to recognize a healthy relationship at all. Sometimes, when the mind is confused, the body can bring you clarity. In this exercise, you will explore ways your body lets you know if a relationship is healthy or not.

Think of a relationship you consider toxic. Bring up a picture of the other person in your mind, or recall a memory of a negative interaction with that person. Don't go to the worst memory you have. Instead, think of an upsetting, but not overwhelming, memory. When you have the memory firmly in your mind, answer the following questions:

What emotions do you experience when you think about this person or the interaction?

_____

_____

_____

What does your body feel like as you think about this person or the interaction? Pay attention to your breathing (rapid and shallow, or slow and deep?), tension in your muscles (clenched jaw or hands?), pain or stiffness (sudden headache?), or other sensations (butterflies in the stomach?).

_____

_____

_____

What kind of posture do you instinctively adopt when you think about this person? Do you want to curl up in a ball, hide under the table, or raise your fists?

_____

_____

Choose a bodily sensation to focus on, such as posture, tension, pain, or breathing. You may close your eyes, if you wish. Pay attention to the sensation, and notice what emotions come up as you concentrate on your body. What feelings are connected to your physical response?

_____

_____

_____

_____

Now think about the *healthiest* relationship in your life. Fix an image of the other person firmly in your mind, and pull up a memory of when you felt loved, supported, validated, or cared for. What emotions come up with this memory?

_____

_____

_____

What does your body feel like as you think about this person and this interaction? Pay attention to your breathing, tension or relaxation in your muscles, pain or stiffness, and any other bodily sensations.

_____

_____

_____

What kind of posture do you instinctively adopt when you think about this person?

_____

_____

_____

Choose a bodily sensation to focus on, such as posture, tension, pain, or breathing. You may close your eyes, if you wish. Pay attention to the sensation, and notice what emotions come up as you concentrate on your body. What feelings are connected to your physical response?

_____

_____

_____

What differences do you notice in the way your body responds to thinking about a toxic relationship versus a healthy one? How can you use your body's messages to assess whether a relationship is healthy?

_____

_____

_____

Resetting Unrealistic Expectations

Sometimes, a person who has experienced many toxic relationships has a hard time knowing how to handle relationship problems productively. With toxic friends, family, and other relationship partners, they may excuse too much abusive behavior in the hopes the behavior will one day stop. Or, they may have the understandable—but ultimately unrealistic—expectation that healthy relationships mean no one gets hurt.

The truth is, we all relate to each other as flawed, imperfect humans. Mistakes and missteps will happen. We may expect too much of some, and too little of others. This exercise helps you explore some of the common unrealistic expectations that can lead to hurt and disappointment in relationships.

Unrealistic Expectation #1: My partner will complete me as a person.

Realistic Reset #1: I am a complete person by myself. My partner and I complement each other, but neither of us needs the other to be whole.

Ways this unrealistic expectation has shown up for me:

_____

_____

_____

_____

_____

Unrealistic Expectation #2: Setting the right boundaries will make my person in this relationship stop treating me so poorly.

Realistic Reset #2: Boundaries define my actions, choices, and tolerance. I cannot change someone else, only myself.

Ways this unrealistic expectation has shown up for me:

_____

_____

_____

_____

_____

Unrealistic Expectation #3: If my loved one is upset with me, I owe it to them to make them feel better.

Realistic Reset #3: I am responsible for my feelings and behaviors, and my loved one is responsible for theirs. I can feel compassion for my loved one's feelings without taking on the responsibility of those feelings.

Ways this unrealistic expectation has shown up for me:

_____

_____

_____

_____

Unrealistic Expectation #4: Love means never having to say you're sorry. (Sorry, *Love Story*.)

Realistic Reset #4: If I truly hurt or wrong someone, even if unintentional, I care enough to take responsibility and try to make it right.

Ways this unrealistic expectation has shown up for me:

_____

_____

_____

_____

Unrealistic Expectation #5: A really healthy relationship will never bring me pain.

Realistic Reset #5: We are all human, and all make mistakes. I don't expect perfection, and I know I will make mistakes, too.

Ways this unrealistic expectation has shown up for me:

_____

_____

_____

_____

Healthy Relationship Models in Pop Culture

Many of the relationships portrayed in film, TV, and celebrity culture are less than healthy. Some, however, serve as models of healthy relationships in action. Here are a few positive examples:

- Ben Wyatt and Leslie Knope in *Parks and Recreation* (dating and marital)
- River and Simon Tam in *Firefly* and *Serenity* (siblings)
- Cameron and Mitchell in *Modern Family* (marital)
- Elizabeth and Henry McCord in *Madam Secretary* (marital)
- Ted and Marshall in *How I Met Your Mother* (friends)
- Harry and Hermione in the Harry Potter series (friends)
- The Hobbits in *Lord of the Rings* (friends)
- Juno and Mac in *Juno* (child and parent)
- The Johnson family in *Black-ish* (family)
- The Pearsons in *This Is Us* (family)

What other examples can you think of? Write them here:

_____

_____

_____

_____

_____

_____

_____

_____

_____

_____

_____

_____

_____

_____

_____

Healthy Relationship Benefits

How does participating in healthy relationships actually help you? The list below outlines some of the benefits of healthy, positive relationships. Add your own below!

- Healthy relationships promote physical health.
- Healthy relationships improve mental health.
- Healthy relationships boost confidence, security, and self-esteem.
- Healthy relationships allow members to experience and resolve conflicts without irreparably rupturing the connection.
- Healthy relationships support members through significant life transitions such as births, deaths, marriages, divorces, and career changes.
- Healthy relationships among parents benefit children in a family.

Additional benefits of healthy relationships:

_____

_____

_____

_____

_____

Healthy Relationship Behaviors

Healthy relationships are created through mind-set, intentions, and actions. Creating a healthy relationship without behaving in ways that promote health is impossible. Below is a list of healthy relationship behaviors. How can you show these in your relationships?

Taking Responsibility for Your Own Thoughts, Feelings, and Behaviors
I can show this responsibility by:

_____

_____

_____

_____

Communicating Assertively

I can show this assertiveness by:

_____

_____

_____

_____

_____

_____

Participating and Collaborating with Peers and Colleagues

I can show this participation and collaboration by:

_____

_____

_____

_____

_____

_____

_____

Respecting Others' Boundaries

I can show this respect by:

_____

_____

_____

_____

_____

Having Realistic Expectations

I can show having realistic expectations by:

_____

_____

_____

_____

Being Consistent and Reliable

I can show this consistence and reliability by:

_____

_____

_____

_____

Supporting Loved Ones

I can show this support by:

_____

_____

_____

_____

_____

Showing Appreciation

I can show this appreciation by:

_____

_____

_____

_____

Nurturing What You Have

To develop healthier, stronger relationships, valuing and nurturing the ones you already have is critically important. A solid friendship, family relationship, work relationship, or intimate relationship can be an invaluable support as you work to heal from a toxic relationship. Don't take the people in your life who love and support you for granted. What are some ways you can nurture your positive relationships?

Spend Time Together.
There is no substitute for actually spending time with someone who cares about you. Don't allow yourself to be "too busy" to spend time with loved ones. If being in the same place physically is not an option, carve out time for a phone or video call. Beware the temptation to put off the time you put in because you know the other person will always be there for you. Relationships thrive when you put the time and energy into feeding them.

Identify at least one opportunity to spend time in a positive relationship this week.

_____

_____

_____

_____

_____

Express Gratitude and Appreciation.
A truly loving and supportive relationship is worth more than gold, but sometimes we forget to express our thanks and appreciation for those who have been with us all along. Don't assume your loved ones know how you feel—make *sure* they know!

Identify at least one thing you can express appreciation for in a positive relationship.

_____

_____

_____

_____

_____

Offer Your Support.

You may feel like you're always asking for support, and never strong enough to give it. Healthy relationships are based on give-and-take, even if the giving and taking look different. Perhaps one person shows support by offering a shoulder to cry on, while another shows support by cooking a meal for a grieving loved one. How can you support your loved ones?

Identify at least one way you can offer support in a loving relationship.

_____

_____

_____

_____

_____

Prioritize Your Healthy Relationships.

Focusing most of your time and energy on the relationships you want to improve or escape can be tempting. There is value in putting the time and energy into improving a relationship by setting boundaries, communicating more assertively, and taking better care of yourself. But equally, if not more, important is to give energy to making sure healthy relationships thrive. Relationships placed on a back burner are at risk of atrophy. How can you prioritize the relationships that feed and support you?

Identify at least one opportunity to prioritize a healthy relationship this week.

_____

_____

_____

_____

_____

_____

_____

Recognizing the Patterns

Very often, the hurtful relationship dynamics you experience in the present have roots in hurtful past experiences. Throughout this workbook, you have identified and explored the beliefs and relationship models that led you to the unhealthy relationships you are now working on healing. Here, you will put the pieces together to identify the cycle that has brought you back to unhealthy relationships time and time again.

The Relationship Blueprints with Which You Started

Think back to the relationship history exercises you completed in chapters 3, 4, and 5. Using what you learned about your family relationships, outline what you were taught about how relationships look, feel, and work. This forms the basis of the relationship blueprint with which you started.

Example: *My relationship blueprint was watching my parents fight constantly. They hit below the belt, and whoever hurt the other one most was the winner. That taught me that cruelty in relationships was normal.*

My relationship blueprint:

_____

_____

_____

_____

The Self-Beliefs That Make You Vulnerable

Review all the exercises in chapters 2, 3, 4, and 5 exploring the way your beliefs about yourself have made you vulnerable to gaslighting. Summarize the beliefs you hold (or previously held) about yourself that have contributed to being victimized in toxic relationships.

My self-beliefs:

_____

_____

_____

_____

_____

_____

The Self-Concept That Keeps You Stuck

In chapters 3, 4, and 5, you explored how your self-perception may keep you stuck in negative relationships. In chapter 6, you identified barriers to self-care that may contribute to stagnation. Summarize how your self-concept may have kept you stuck in toxic relationships.

My self-concept:

_____

_____

_____

_____

_____

The Abuses You Have Tolerated

Toxic relationships continue because one party has been willing or conditioned to overlook, excuse, or tolerate abusive behavior. In chapters 1 and 2, you learned what gaslighting is, what drives a gaslighter, and what makes gaslightees vulnerable to abuse. Summarize what you have learned about abuse in your toxic relationships.

Abuse I have tolerated:

_____

_____

_____

_____

_____

Breaking the Cycle

Now that you have a clear picture of the negative patterns and cycles of your unhealthy relationships, it is time to break the cycle. For each piece of the toxic relationship, identify one opportunity to break the cycle.

Example: *My relationship blueprint was based on watching my parents fight and be cruel to each other. I can change the blueprint by choosing to fight fair or to walk away from a relationship where cruelty is normal.*

Changing the Blueprint

One way I can change the blueprint is:

_____

_____

_____

Checking the Self-Beliefs That Made Me Vulnerable

One way I can check a self-belief that made me vulnerable is:

_____

_____

_____

Challenging the Self-Concept That Kept Me Stuck

One self-concept I can challenge is:

_____

_____

_____

Choosing Not to Accept the Abuse

One way I can choose not to accept continued abuse is:

_____

_____

_____

Don't Take the Bait

Gaslighters keep victims trapped by making them believe they can't trust the evidence of their senses. They control their victims by overriding the victim's sense of having been treated badly, keeping them trapped in a harmful cycle. If a victim does gain enough self-confidence to stay firm and call out the toxic behavior, gaslighters may switch tactics and promise to change their behavior. Unfortunately, in abusive relationships, this promise is not made with an honest intention of self-improvement.

Rather, the empty words serve only to suck victims back into the relationship at a point where they might have broken the cycle.

In the deepest levels of the ocean, there is a creature called an anglerfish that lures prey into its jaws by dangling a small, glowing light in front of its teeth. Like an anglerfish drawing victims in with a false promise of light in the deep, gaslighters lure victims back in with promises to change.

How have you been lured back into abusive relationships in your life?

_____

_____

_____

_____

_____

_____

_____

How can you make yourself immune to the allure of a false promise? What do you need to tell yourself to resist the lure of the light?

_____

_____

_____

_____

_____

_____

_____

_____

_____

Toxic Behavior Can Be Unintentional

What if I told you that toxic behavior can take place without abusive intent? The fact is, not all negative relationship behaviors are necessarily abusive. Even kind, loving, compassionate people can engage in unhealthy behaviors. They may not even be aware of what they're doing.

In relationships that are unintentionally hurtful, there is a reasonable chance the other person will show some willingness and motivation to learn healthier behaviors. They will respect your boundaries and accept responsibility for their actions. In an abusive relationship, the other person will not respect your boundaries, and will place the blame on you.

We are all products of our environment as well as our inherent personalities. While many people may certainly seek to control others for their own benefit, many engage in unhealthy behaviors simply because they don't know any other way to act. Sometimes the only way we learn healthy relationship behaviors is to suffer the consequences of our unhealthy behaviors.

Think about the relationships in your life that have been characterized by unhealthy patterns and behaviors. Can you identify any that may have been unintentionally harmful, as opposed to willfully abusive?

Check Yourself for Fleas

There is an old saying that goes like this: "Lie down with dogs and you'll get up with fleas." Though perhaps not the most charming phrase, it does have a core of truth. Over time, people who have been in toxic relationships may find themselves engaging in toxic behavior themselves. Victims of abuse may feel like the only way to gain power, or to avoid being victimized again, is to turn the toxic behavior against the other person. Be gentle, but mindful, of potential fleas in your own behavior.

THE ART OF THE APOLOGY

If you have been gaslit into apologizing when you did nothing wrong, you might feel understandably reluctant to complete an exercise about apologies. I encourage you to do it, anyway. Neither person in a healthy relationship, as we have previously discussed, can completely avoid making mistakes and hurting their partner. Knowing when and how to make a sincere apology is key to creating and nurturing healthy relationships.

An effective apology is:

Timely. A good apology is offered at the right time. Ideally, you apologize immediately; if you only find out later that you hurt someone, offer the apology as soon as you find out.

Sincere. "Sorry/not sorry" is not an apology. Neither is "I'm sorry, but . . ." Offer an apology only if you can do so sincerely and honestly, without trying to rationalize or justify your actions.

Needed in cases of true wrongdoing or hurt. An apology is not necessary when you have not actually done anything wrong. Gaslighters will try to make you apologize for things that are not your responsibility. Don't take the bait.

Focused on your own actions. If you *have* done something that wrongs or harms another person, focus your apology on what you did. Even if the other person did something to precipitate your act, your apology should be focused on your own choices.

A promise to do better. A good apology recognizes that you did something wrong and expresses a commitment to avoid hurting the other person in this way again. Apologies should indicate your intention to be more healthy, loving, and compassionate as your relationship grows.

The Most Important Relationship in Your Life

What is the most important relationship you have now, or will ever have?

_____

_____

_____

Describe your relationship with yourself.

_____

_____

_____

Much of this workbook has been focused on helping you rebuild your relationship with yourself. Gaslighting separates you from your sense of self and causes you to distrust yourself. In order to create healthier relationships moving forward, you must first recreate a connection to yourself.

Review the self-care exercises in chapter 6. Just as you need to put energy into nurturing healthy relationships so they can thrive, you need to put energy into restoring your relationship with yourself. Write yourself a letter of promise, speaking your intention to rediscover, nourish, and deepen your relationship with yourself. You deserve your own love, care, compassion, and commitment.

My Letter of Commitment:

_____

_____

_____

_____

_____

_____

_____

_____

_____

_____

_____

_____

_____

_____

_____

_____

_____

_____

_____

_____

_____

_____

Healthy Relationship Affirmation

Create at least three mantras to call abundance in healthy relationships into your life. Remember to speak with confidence that you will receive what you seek.

Examples:

I am grateful for the love and support of my relationships.

I appreciate the people around me, who care for me and build me up.

I welcome health and growth in my relationships.

Your Turn:

_____

_____

_____

_____

_____

_____

_____

Review and Wrap-Up

Look back at the exercises in this chapter.

What resonated with you the most?

_____

_____

_____

_____

_____

_____

_____

What did not resonate?

_____

_____

_____

_____

_____

_____

_____

_____

How do you feel right now? Have your feelings changed since you started this chapter?

_____

_____

_____

_____

_____

_____

_____

What will you take away from these exercises?

_____

_____

_____

_____

_____

_____

A FINAL WORD

Congratulations on completing the *Gaslighting Recovery Workbook*! In working through these exercises, you have taken your first steps toward a healthier life. Some chapters and exercises were likely harder than others; you should be very proud of yourself for working through them. If there were any exercises or sections you found too difficult or triggering to work through, I encourage you to try again with the support of a great therapist. Remember: Seeking help is not a sign of failure, but the simple acknowledgment that you need some added support.

I wish I could say that completing this workbook means all your relationships will henceforth be healthy, fulfilling, and satisfying. Unfortunately, I can't make that promise. But I *can* say that by working through these exercises, you have created the possibility for growth, change, and healing as well as the possibility of a whole new life.

As a result of your work to heal and recover, you will walk into new relationships with a different sense of your worth and value. You will be more prepared to expect fair treatment, and less likely to fall prey to abusive people. If you do find yourself in a toxic relationship, you will be better equipped to disengage and disrupt the cycle. You will be better able to practice self-care, self-compassion, and self-kindness.

I am so proud of you, dear reader, for your dedication to your healing and recovery. You are strong, brave, and resilient. You deserve—and are capable of creating—loving, strong, and healthy relationships. Good luck to you as you begin the next chapter of your life feeling stronger, more confident, and more wholly You.

I wish you joy, hope, and healing.

RESOURCES

NATIONAL THERAPIST REGISTRIES

GoodTherapy,
www.goodtherapy.org

The International Resource Center for Daughters, Sons and Partners of Narcissists,
www.willieverbegoodenough.com/resources/find-a-therapist

National Queer & Trans Therapists of Color Network,
www.nqttcn.com/directory

Open Path Psychotherapy Collective,
www.openpathcollective.org

Psychology Today,
www.psychologytoday.com

Therapy for Black Girls,
www.therapyforblackgirls.com

TherapyTribe,
www.therapytribe.com

Theravive,
www.theravive.com

WEBSITES

The International Resource Center for Daughters, Sons and Partners of Narcissists,
www.willieverbegoodenough.com

Luke 17:3 Ministries,
www.luke173ministries.org

Narcissist Abuse Support,
www.narcissistabusesupport.com

Out of the FOG,
www.outofthefog.website

BOOKS

The Body Keeps the Score: Brain, Mind, and Body in the Healing of Trauma, by Bessel van der Kolk. 2014.

Boundaries: When to Say Yes, How to Say No to Take Control of Your Life, by Henry Cloud & John Townsend. 1992.

Gaslighting: Recognize Manipulative and Emotionally Abusive People—And Break Free, by Stephanie Sarkis. 2018.

Healing from Hidden Abuse: A Journey through the Stages of Recovery from Psychological Abuse, by Shannon Thomas. 2016.

REFERENCES

CHAPTER ONE: WHAT IS GASLIGHTING?

Dictionary.com. "What Does Gaslighting Mean?" Accessed August 23, 2019. https://www.dictionary.com/e/pop-culture/gaslighting.

A Gaslit Society

Beerbohm, Eric, and Ryan Davis. "Gaslighting Citizens." Accessed August 21, 2019. Beerbohm Harvard Files. https://scholar.harvard.edu/files/beerbohm/files/eb_rd_gaslighting_citizens_apsa_2018_v1_1_0.pdf.

The Social Media and Advertising Effect

Shah, Saqib. "The History of Social Networking." Digital Trends. May 14, 2016. https://www.digitaltrends.com/features/the-history-of-social-networking.

Signs of Gaslighting

Sarkis, Stephanie. "How to Cope with a Gaslighting or Narcissist Boss." *Forbes*. March 29, 2019. https://www.forbes.com/sites/stephaniesarkis/2019/03/29/coping-with-a-gaslighting-or-narcissist-boss/#1b4aa7046097.

CHAPTER TWO: THE GASLIGHTER

Schouten, Ronald, and James Silver. *Almost a Psychopath: Do I (or Does Someone I Know) Have a Problem with Manipulation and Lack of Empathy? (The Almost Effect)*. Center City, MN: Hazelden Publishing, 2012.

Profile of the Abuser

National Institute of Mental Health. "Personality Disorders." Last updated November 2017. https://www.nimh.nih.gov/health/statistics/personality-disorders.shtml.

Narcissistic Personality Disorder; Borderline Personality Disorder

American Psychiatric Association. "What Are Personality Disorders?" November 2018. https://www.psychiatry.org/patients-families/personality-disorders/what-are-personality-disorders.

Other Sociopathic Disorders

Tracy, Natasha. "Psychopath vs Sociopath: What's the Difference?" HealthyPlace. Last updated May 31, 2019. https://www.healthyplace.com/personality-disorders/psychopath/psychopath-vs-sociopath-what-s-the-difference.

Understanding Gaslighting Behavior

Sarkis, Stephanie. *Gaslighting: Recognize Manipulative and Emotionally Abusive People—And Break Free*. New York: Da Capo Press, 2018.

Dodgson, Lindsay. "Psychological Abusers Don't Go for the Weak—They Choose Strong People because They 'Like a Challenge.'" *Business Insider*. Aug. 11, 2017. https://www.businessinsider.com/strong-confident-people-end-up-in-abusive-relationships-2017-8.

CHAPTER THREE: PHASE ONE (ACKNOWLEDGMENT AND SELF-COMPASSION)

Gaslighting in a Vulnerable Population

National Domestic Violence Hotline. "LGBTQ Relationship Violence." Accessed Aug. 24, 2019. https://www.thehotline.org/is-this-abuse/lgbt-abuse/.

When the Body Speaks, Listen

Van der Kolk, Bessel. *The Body Keeps the Score: Brain, Mind, and Body in the Healing of Trauma*. New York: Penguin Books, 2014.

Emotional Abuse Is Not Gendered

National Domestic Violence Hotline. "Get the Facts and Figures." Accessed Aug. 24, 2019. https://www.thehotline.org/resources/statistics/.

Self-Compassion Journal

Neff, Kristin. "Exercise Six: Self-Compassion Journal." Accessed Aug. 25, 2019. https://self-compassion.org/exercise-6-self-compassion-journal/.

Noticing Compassion Daily Log

Adapted from: ACT with Compassion. "Self-Compassion Daily Rating Scale." Accessed Aug. 25, 2019. https://www.actwithcompassion.com/noticing_compassion_daily_reflection.

Adapted from Neff, Kristen. "Test How Self-Compassionate You Are." Accessed Oct. 30, 2019. https://self-compassion.org/test-how-self-compassionate-you-are/.

CHAPTER FOUR: PHASE TWO (ASSERTIVENESS)

Assertive Bill of Rights

Adapted from: Smith, Manuel J. *When I Say No, I Feel Guilty*. New York: Bantam Books, 1975.

Positive Traits Experienced

Therapist Aid. (blog). "Positive Traits Worksheet." Accessed Aug. 29, 2019. https://www.therapistaid.com/therapy-worksheet/positive-traits/self-esteem/none. History of Growth Timeline (blank timeline template): https://www.smartsheet.com/sites/default/files/styles/full_width_desktop/public/IC-Horizontal-Blank-Timeline-Template-PDF.jpg?itok=mN88PhIy.

Communication Styles

Alvernia University. (blog). "4 Types of Communication Styles." Mar. 27, 2018. https://online.alvernia.edu/articles/4-types-communication-styles/.

I-Statements

Therapist Aid. (blog). "I-Statements Worksheet." Accessed Aug. 30, 2019. https://www.therapistaid.com/therapy-worksheet/i-statements.

Fears of a People-Pleaser

Adapted from: Anderson, Frank G., Martha Sweezy, and Richard C. Schwartz. *Internal Family Systems Skills Training Manual: Trauma-Informed Treatment for Anxiety, Depression, PTSD, & Substance Abuse.* Eau Claire, WI: PESI Publishing & Media, 2017.

The Benefits of Assertiveness

Mayo Clinic Staff. "Being Assertive: Reduce Stress, Communicate Better." May 9, 2017. https://www.mayoclinic.org/healthy-lifestyle/stress-management/in-depth/assertive/art-20044644.

CHAPTER FIVE: PHASE THREE (ESTABLISHING BOUNDARIES)

Boundary Drawing Exercise

http://arttherapydirectives.blogspot.com/2012/07/boundary-drawings.html.

Guilt Messages Unmasked

The Boundaries Books Team. (blog). "How to Handle Guilt Messages from Your Mom." Oct. 8, 2018. https://www.boundariesbooks.com/boundaries/handle-guilt-messages-from-your-mom/.

Levels of Contact

Martin, Sharon. "How to Set Boundaries with Toxic People." Accessed Sept. 2, 2019. https://narcissistabusesupport.com/set-boundaries-toxic-people/.

CHAPTER SIX: SELF-CARE

Physical Self-Care: Rest, Recover, and Refresh

Dickinson, Elizabeth Evitts. "The Cult of Busy." *Johns Hopkins Health Review* 3, no. 1 (Spring/Summer 2016).

Physical Self-Care: Get Moving

Centers for Disease Control and Prevention. "Physical Activity Is for Everybody." Last updated Oct. 18, 2017. https://www.cdc.gov/features/physical-activity-disabilities/index.html.
Mayo Clinic Staff. "Fibromyalgia: Does Exercise Help or Hurt?" Nov. 11, 2016. https://www.mayoclinic.org/diseases-conditions/fibromyalgia/in-depth/fibromyalgia
-and-exercise/art-20093376.

Emotional Self-Care: Heal and Release

Anderson, Frank G., Martha Sweezy, and Richard C. Schwartz. *Internal Family Systems Skills Training Manual: Trauma-Informed Treatment for Anxiety, Depression, PTSD, & Substance Abuse*. Eau Claire, WI: PESI Publishing & Media, 2017.
Austen, Brad. "Healing the Heart Guided Meditation." Accessed Sept. 22, 2019. https://www.exploremeditation.com/healing-heart-meditation-script/.

Self-Care Is Necessary for Healing

Arabi, Shahida. "5 Powerful Self-Care Practices That Can Save Your Life after Emotional Abuse." November 18, 2017. https://thoughtcatalog.com/shahida-arabi/2017/11/5
-powerful-ways-to-rise-again-after-emotional-abuse/.

Introvert/Extravert

The Myers & Briggs Foundation. "Extraversion or Introversion." Accessed Sept. 24, 2019. https://www.myersbriggs.org/my-mbti-personality-type/mbti-basics/extraversion
-or-introversion.htm?bhcp=1.

10 Ideas for Self-Care Activities

Centers for Disease Control and Prevention. "About Pets & People." Last reviewed Apr. 15, 2019. Accessed Sept. 23, 2019. https://www.cdc.gov/healthypets/health-benefits/index.html.

CHAPTER SEVEN: ESTABLISHING HEALTHY RELATIONSHIPS

Qualities of Healthy Relationships

Hall Health Center Hall Promotion Staff. "Healthy vs. Unhealthy Relationships." University of Washington. Accessed Sept. 22, 2019. http://depts.washington.edu/hhpccweb/health-resource/healthy-vs-unhealthy-relationships/.
University of Washington. (blog). "Healthy Relationships." Accessed Sept. 22, 2019. https://depts.washington.edu/livewell/advocate/healthy-relationships/.

Resetting Unrealistic Expectations

Rutherford-Morrison, Lara. "5 Ways Couples with Realistic Expectations Are Happier, More in Love, and Have Better Relationships." June 3, 2015. https://www.bustle.com/articles
/87084-5-ways-couples-with-realistic-expectations-are-happier-more-in-love-and-have-
better-relationships.

Healthy Relationship Benefits

VA San Diego Healthcare System. "10 Things You Should Know about Healthy Family Functioning." Accessed Sept. 26, 2019. https://www.ruralhealth.va.gov/docs/ruralclergytraining/family-functioning.pdf.

Check Yourself for Fleas

Out of the FOG. (blog). "What Not to Do: Fleas." Accessed Sept. 27, 2019. https://outofthefog.website/what-not-to-do-1/2015/12/3/fleas.

The Art of the Apology

Lerner, Harriet. "The 9 Rules for True Apologies." *Psychology Today*. Sept. 14, 2014. https://www.psychologytoday.com/us/blog/the-dance-connection/201409/the-9-rules-true-apologies.

INDEX

ACKNOWLEDGMENTS

I want to begin by thanking the people who have always known this day would come: my mother and my late father. Thank you, Mom and Dad, for never doubting that I would one day become an author. Thank you for your encouragement to keep writing, and for believing that I could fulfill my dream of helping people. Dad, I know you would be so proud.

Thank you to my friends and colleagues, who cheered me on and celebrated each milestone with me. Amy, Kristen, and Marysel, I am so grateful for your love, encouragement, and support.

Thank you to my clients. You have taught me the nature of resiliency and strength. You are wonderful.

Dr. Marjory Levitt, thank you for teaching me that the heart of healing is in the relationship. Thank you for training, guiding, and supporting a fledgling therapist.

To Caelyn and Eleanor, my beautiful and amazing daughters, thank you for your patience with my busyness. Everything I do is in the hope of creating a better life, and a better world, for you to grow up in. I love you both so much.

Finally, to my husband, Tom. There aren't enough words to express my love, appreciation, and gratitude for having you in my life. Thank you for loving, supporting, encouraging, and challenging me. Thank you for your patience. And thank you for taking on the lion's share of the childcare so I could write this workbook. I love you, I love you, I love you.

ABOUT THE AUTHOR

Amy Marlow-MaCoy is a licensed professional counselor. With compassion, empathy, and an unapologetically nerdy sense of humor, Amy writes about the hard things in life: emotional abuse, relationships, and healing. Amy draws from her experience as a therapist specializing in supporting survivors of narcissistic abuse to help individuals heal and recover from gaslighting in relationships. When not engaged in the work of healing hearts, Amy is usually either lost in a sci-fi novel, snuggling with her cats, or perfecting her deadlift.

CPSIA information can be obtained
at www.ICGtesting.com
Printed in the USA
BVHW021819010421
603948BV00025B/456

9 781646 112692